The
Vicar's
Wife's
Cook Book

Danny & Karen,
Thank you for your friendship.
very Best Wishes
Steve & Agnes Yafai xx
27 March 2009.

The
Vicar's
Wife's
Cook Book
Elisa Beynon

FOURTH ESTATE · London

First published in Great Britain in 2009 by
Fourth Estate
A division of HarperCollinsPublishers
77–85 Fulham Palace Road
London W6 8JB
www.4thestate.co.uk

love this book? www.bookarmy.com

A catalogue record for this book is available from the British Library

ISBN 978-0-00-727612-7

Typeset in Caslon by Envy Design

Printed and bound in Great Britain by Butler Tanner and Dennis Ltd,
Frome, Somerset

For my N

The Vicar's Wife, Elisa Beynon, is a wonderful new voice in British food writing, bringing humour, wit and a good dose of real-life living back to daily cooking.

Winner of the hotly contested competition run by *Waitrose Food Illustrated* and Fourth Estate in 2007 Elisa's entry impressed the judges with its witty and refreshingly honest approach to food.

Banishing all mention of jam-making sprees and village fêtes, Elisa really considers what people at her table would most like to eat. Individuals are drawn in around the kitchen table; dishes are designed to please and food is made to be shared.

As thrifty, hard-working mother of two, Elisa shows how accessible ingredients and a busy family kitchen can be managed to impressively stress-free effect to help you relish feeding the ones you care about without costing an arm and a leg.

Contents

Acknowledgements

I know not many people read these bits and I have to confess that the times I have bothered, I have sometimes felt a sense of irritation. The endless eulogies occasionally make me wonder if the author has transported him- or herself to an Oscar ceremony. However, I am now forced to play the hypocrite. I feel very privileged to have been given the chance to write this book. And the fact it is actually on the shelves pays tribute to a host of people, some of whom I have known for years, some of whom I have come to know, and others I don't – but they have still played a part. So Oscar gown donned, it's my turn to blub.

All this started with a competition to find a cookery writer, launched by *Waitrose Food Illustrated*. How glad I am that, standing in a queue at the supermarket, I picked up the in-store magazine. To the panel of judges who chose me (you fools!) I thank you. That's William Sitwell, Louise Haines, Claire Paterson, Tif Loehnis and Nigel Slater.

Louise Haines became my editor. I was told she is the best in the business. I have no knowledge of other editors but personally think she is the bee's knees. I thank her particularly for her unending patience with my constant worrying and well, just the calm way she does everything. I have tried to stop myself wishing I was more like her. And have sometimes failed.

Also a big thank you to everyone at 4th Estate: Jessica Axe, Julian Humphries, Elizabeth Woabank and Jo Walker. I didn't know very much about publishing before but I feel very fortunate to be supported by such a talented bunch. And they are sweet and fun as well as clever.

Claire Paterson became my agent – the poor girl. In private I call her Doctor Claire as I normally call her in a spin and she prescribes the right medicine.

And Nigel Slater – turns out he is as lovely as his recipes. Of course we all knew that. But I now can tell you, personally – it's true. He has been immensely kind and encouraging.

And to all at *WFI* – fab shop; fab magazine.

See, it's already Oscar-gushy. I apologise. There's a bit more to come.

My wonderful friends. Many of them (with vicars' wives amongst them) have helped me in this book. Either in recipe testing, suggestions, or practical support. I send thanks to:

The Mortimers
Clara (Clare Jackson)
Sue Watts
Kate Chitty
Rebecca and Shane Burford-Lewis
Ray Dosser
Rachel Brabner
Sue McGowan
My out-laws
Juliette Shelley
Liz and Drew
Adam and Alexia and Helen and Simon and Mark and Nicole
Sweet Caroline

My local shops
Alex the Caff
Liz and Marie in the Dry Cleaners

Particular foodie thanks:

I am a home cook; I am not a trained chef. This thanks bubbles over to thanking 4th Estate again, because to them I owe meeting Debbie Major and Jane Middleton. They stepped in on timings when my oven was idiotic and they made things work. And they were also really nice.

Thanks too, to Helena Caldon. Her husband's family hails from Beynon stock – a nice touch. And she has done a wonderful job at reining in any nonsense in the text.

I also want to thank my mother. She is a small little thing – but came in the last days of the book to clean the fridge and mop up damp chaos. Thank you, little Mam.

But of course, my biggest thanks goes to the Vicar, who is actually not an active vicar as I write but I can't help but call him that.

Without him, this book would never have happened. (So if you don't like it, blame him.) More seriously, he has been encouraging, kind, patient, gentle and loving … even when I've been a ratty old bag.

Thank you, my dearest N.

Introduction

If you don't like being around food, it isn't the best idea in the world to marry a vicar …

Back in early 2007, idly standing at the check-out in Waitrose, my eye chanced upon a headline on their in-store magazine. 'Win a £20,000 book deal.'

It didn't sound such a bad idea.

Back at home, I showed the Vicar the article. Written by Nigel Slater, it put out a plea for a new food writer; someone who could give even him a run for his money. (Yeah, right.) The Vicar, bored silly of years of my dreamily droning on about writing a cookery book, literally begged me to enter. Here, at last, was something to galvanise his unmotivated little wife into action.

A few months and a fair few recipes later, I found out that I'd won – and I haven't stopped pinching myself since. Untrained, I only learnt to cook because marrying the Vicar necessitated some sort of culinary provision for passing guests. However, I beg you, do not misunderstand me here; I didn't *have* to learn. The Vicar is a very gentle man and he would never have forced me into an apron and frog-marched me into the kitchen, but, somehow, being with him did propel me towards the stove.

For a start, we couldn't afford to buy take-aways for all our many visitors; and secondly, I wanted to make him happy and look after him a bit. The poor man married me the year my father died, and he was a triumph at mopping me up and patiently being there as I struggled to cope. The very least I could offer in return was a nice hot dinner at the end of a long day. However, whilst my initial forays in the kitchen may have been altruistic, I confess it didn't stay that way for long. Very gradually, from being someone who counted Fruit Pastilles as part of her five-a-day, food and cooking began to excite me. I didn't have a house packed with cook books; I didn't have the best kitchen gadgets or the finest fridge-freezer; but I did have eyes to explore the delights of fresh produce, a nose (and mine is quite large) to sniff and savour, and hands to explore, examine and touch. Over time, and very many little messes, I began to understand the beauty of marrying different flavours: how chillies and limes are a match made in heaven, and that when cumin met lamb it was love at first sight.

Not only that, I found that whilst cooking made me happy, it made others happy, too. As someone who is indecently protective of friendship and relationships, this was addictive stuff. Having people over and letting them know through the food that I prepared for them that I loved them and cared for them, was, and is, a wonderful thing. I am not the most practical of people, and at times I forget to return calls or write a thank-you note, but I can manage to put my mind to the person who is coming to my house and ponder what this friend would really like to eat.

Unlike animals, food is more to us than mere fodder: meals feature in those memories we have that evoke a passion, a sense of comfort, or a feeling of calm. And I confess that when I cook for friends and family, my longing is to provide something that will ignite a spark. I want to give them something personal and say, on a dinner plate, 'I love you, you know.' It might be grazing food for a love-sick friend or sausages and mash for a hearty lad, but in everything I cook, I want it to send a message.

As a result, this book is quite personal. I talk about people I know – and love – very much. And, yes, I have planned the recipes around them. As you turn the pages of this book you will undoubtedly pick up that the Vicar loves lamb and that I do try to find out my guests' food likes and dislikes before they arrive at my table. As eating is, for me, inextricably linked to the people I shared it all with, I have also included a few anecdotes along the way. If you want to skip them and move on to how many onions you need, I won't be in the least offended. I offer it all, not to be prescriptive (how dare I?) but, hopefully, to inspire.

Your friends and family may be different from mine, but we all need to remember to relish the people we love and, dare I suggest it, enjoy the delights of feeding them. I hope these recipes will help you to do just that, even a little.

Since ditching vegetarianism some time back, Sunday lunch has come alive for me. Strange, really, that it's eating dead animals that has had this enlivening effect, but there you have it. Every week, as I open the front door on my return from church, I'm transported to a state of salivating expectancy as I get the first sniff of the meal to come. Then, just as I'm finishing the last mouthful of my present lunch, I'm already musing on what meat I will serve next week and wondering which vegetables will be in my mid-week organic delivery box that will both act as the perfect backdrop and the subtle enhancer of my yearned-for protein punch.

Whether we are alone or have guests, the Vicar and I 'do' Sunday lunch with gusto – there's no wimping out for us. It may seem extravagant to buy a whole chicken or a joint for just the two of us and our two small children, but the leftovers can not only provide the wherewithal for a couple more meals in the week ahead, but also a supply of stock for the freezer. Besides, Sunday lunch is a time when it feels especially right to feast as a family around the table: not only does it build mealtime memories in the children's minds that they can (hopefully) treasure in the future, it also, in the present, has the power to hold back, for a few more hours, that gloomy end-of-the-weekend depression.

For myself and the Vicar, though, Sunday lunch is also the time when we have to recognise that, to our confusion and shame, we do indeed have a touch of the churchy stereotype about us. The Vicar may have recently switched roles (after many years in a parish he has now taken up the challenge of conference directing), but nevertheless, as I cook we still pour ourselves and, yes, really enjoy, a small glass of sherry.

Sunday Lunch

Spring and summer

It's easy to think that Sunday lunch has to mean hearty, steaming plates of red meat and crispy roast potatoes on cold, wet days, however, the warmer months still lend themselves to a good old Sunday feed-up – albeit cooked with a lighter touch. It's time to leave behind the earthier flavours of winter and embrace the sprightlier tastes of spring: time to feast on Jersey Royals, hunt for baby broad beans and eschew nursery puddings for airier, berry-laden concoctions. Mind you, our so-called seasons can never be relied upon, so if, on a cold and rainy June day, a plate of roast beef and Yorkshire pud is just what the doctor ordered, then go right ahead and take your medicine …

A lemony lunch

This year the weather has been a hoot: it's only just turned May and it's as though spring has taken a sabbatical and the man behind the weather has fast-tracked us straight into summer. I dreamt up a suitable lunch for this climate – food full of zest and zing, lemons and light – so, brimming with anticipation, I woke up this morning, went downstairs, opened the front door and … it was *cold*. Freezing cold, in fact. Nevertheless, hopeless optimist that I am, I cooked what I had planned and, wonderfully, by the time that we had reached pudding, the sun had come out. Afterwards, as the Arsenal game kicked off, we all hung out of the front door and watched everyone troop past in the warmth. We even spotted a minor celebrity amongst the red-topped fray – and he smiled.

serves 4

I really enjoyed making this lunch, for one rather contemptible reason: it made me feel like the person I, regrettably, am not. That is a tidy, clean-up-as-you-go kind of person; an organised, calm, collected type of cook. For once, I felt this way because this lunch was so pleasurably easy to put together. So if you are naturally a messy little pig like me, make the following for a spritz of zen-like kitchen calm.

The tart needs to be made first to allow time for it to chill: you could even make it the day before.

SPRING-SCENTED CHICKEN

HONEYED BABY CARROTS

JERSEY ROYAL POTATOES IN CHIVES AND BUTTER

A WARM SALAD OF SUMMERY BABY GREEN VEGETABLES

LEMON AND RASPBERRY TART

Spring-scented Chicken

1 organic or free-range chicken,
about 1.5kg
1 lemon
2 tablespoons lemon oil (or ordinary
olive oil if you don't have any)

salt and pepper
8 garlic cloves, peeled but left whole
120ml white wine

Preheat the oven to 200°C/Gas Mark 6. Take your bird, stuff 2 halves of a
lemon up its bottom, and anoint its skin with 2 tablespoons of lemon oil and
lots of salt and pepper. Pop it into a roasting tin, tummy-side down (that is,
breast-side down). I like to start the bird off in this position as I am fanatical
about the breast being as moist as possible, and laying the chicken this way
down encourages the juices to run down into it. You will need to cook the
chicken for around 20 minutes per 500g, plus 30 minutes. Do try and baste it
as and when you remember, too. About halfway through the cooking time,
turn the chicken over so it is tummy-side up.

Meanwhile, take the garlic, put it in a pan of boiling water and let it bubble
away for about 10 minutes or until soft. Drain, reserving the cooking water to
make the sauce, and set aside. Add the garlic to the roasting tin with the chicken
about 20 minutes before it comes out of the oven. When the chicken is done, lift
it onto a big platter, cover it with foil, and put it somewhere warm to rest.

For the light sauce, put the roasting tin on top of the stove and heat it until
the meat juices that are left in it bubble frenetically, and scrape up any sticky
bits stuck to the bottom with a wooden spoon. Crush most of the soft garlic
down into the juices and add the white wine and about 120ml of the reserved
vegetable/garlic water. Let it bubble away until it is reduced and well
flavoured and then add salt and pepper to taste. Keep warm once it's ready.

Honeyed Baby Carrots

about 250g baby carrots
20g butter

1 tablespoon runny honey
salt and pepper

Top and tail the baby carrots and parboil them in boiling, salted water for 5 minutes. Drain, keeping some of the cooking water and adding it to the reserved garlicky water from the chicken.

Put the carrots into a small roasting tin, dot them with butter and sprinkle with some salt and pepper. When the chicken has 40 minutes left of its cooking time, put the carrots in the oven for around 50 minutes, drizzling them with the honey 5 minutes before they are done. This allows time for the carrots to finish cooking while the chicken rests, and gives you a chance to make the light sauce to go with it.

serves 4

Jersey Royal Potatoes in Chives and Butter

500g Jersey Royals, washed
    thoroughly (I like the skins left
    on, but if you dislike that papery
    feel, scrub the potatoes
    thoroughly or peel them)

30g butter
2 tablespoons chives, chopped
salt and pepper

Put a pan of salted boiling water on top of the stove, add the potatoes and leave them to cook for 20–25 minutes, lid on. When they are cooked, drain them and put them back in the hot pan with the butter, chives and lots of salt and pepper.

A Warm Salad of Summery Baby Green Vegetables

100g green beans
about 20 stems of thin baby
    asparagus, trimmed
100g sugar snap peas

For the dressing:
1 garlic clove, peeled and crushed
1 teaspoon French mustard

1 tablespoon lemon juice
3 tablespoons basil oil
2 tablespoons flatleaf parsley,
    chopped
2 tablespoons basil leaves, roughly
    torn
salt and pepper

Throw the beans in a pan of boiling, salted water and cook for about
5 minutes. After 1 minute, add the asparagus. (If you are using the thicker
baby asparagus, you may need to put them in at the same time as the beans.)
Throw in the sugar snaps 3 minutes before the end of the cooking time.

Meanwhile, whisk together the garlic, mustard, lemon juice and basil oil for
the dressing. Stir in the parsley and basil and season to taste with salt and
pepper. Drain the vegetables well, chuck them into a warmed serving dish
and pour over the green herby dressing. Now get everything and everyone to
the table and enjoy all those sunny, fragrant flavours.

serves 4

Lemon and Raspberry Tart

Do feel free to make the pastry for this tart yourself, but if you really can't be bothered with it, do what I did and buy some ready-made fresh pastry. Lazy, I know, but I have a friend at Leith's Cookery School and she confessed to me that pastry was her weak point; and if she is prepared to admit that, then so can you.

250g chilled ready-made sweet pastry
plain flour, for dusting
227g curd or cream cheese
4 tablespoons homemade lemon curd, or a good-quality bought one
finely grated zest of 1 lemon

2 tablespoons pudding wine, such as Muscat de Beaumes de Venise
a big tub of fresh raspberries (about 250g)
icing sugar, to sprinkle

When you have made the pastry, or taken it out of its shop-bought packaging, roll it out thinly on a lightly floured surface and use to line a lightly greased 20cm loose-bottomed flan tin (I used half a packet, so divide in half first). Chill for 20 minutes, then bake it blind – by which I mean you cover it with a sheet of greaseproof paper showered with baking beans.

Bake for 15–20 minutes in an oven preheated to 200°C/Gas Mark 6 until biscuit-coloured, then remove the paper and beans and return to the oven for a further 5 minutes. Once out of the oven, let it cool.

For the filling, combine all the remaining ingredients, bar the raspberries and the icing sugar, until smooth and pour the mixture carefully into the cooled pastry case. Arrange the raspberries on top and then chill for at least 1 hour. Just before serving, put about 1 tablespoon of icing sugar in a big sieve and sprinkle it over the tart. This little touch makes the tart look pretty, and you, professional. (You are welcome to arrange these adjectives the other way around if that makes you feel even better about yourself!)

serves 4   Lemon and Raspberry Tart   13

A very late lunch with the out-laws

Eurovision Song Contest last night. I fell asleep on the sofa, but not before the Vicar had pronounced the show 'a veritable cultural smorgasbord'. Maybe it was that very comment that triggered his suggestion for the next day: as we were on holiday we could do what some crazy non-churchgoers do on a Sunday and go to Ikea. (Not that I'm saying that people who don't go to church are crazy, per se; it's just that Ikea, or anywhere like that, on a Sunday isn't my idea of weekend relaxation.) Anyway, I had idly mentioned I needed a couple of extra things for lunch and he somehow saw it as a chance to go Swedish.

On the way back home I ran into a crowded supermarket to get my stuff and we only got home at around 1pm, the out-laws hot on our heels. They arrived in the rain just as the meat went in; after that, shopping was put away, gin was drunk, jobs were shared out and, very hungrily, we finally ate two hours later.

The meal was perfect for a rainy spring day – the weather was damp enough for us to crave comfort in the form of crackling and mashed potato, but it was too depressing to give up all hope that warmer days were on their way: hence the summery pudding.

As I proved on that late-lunch day, this lot can be cooked in 2 hours flat. Below are the necessaries. I sorted the pork first, then prepared the carrots for the oven, made the mash, got the pudding together and left it on the side, did the pears and then the cabbagey/leeky/fennel stuff and last, but not least, made the gravy/sauce.

Roast pork with crackling and gingered pears

Mustard mash

Roasted carrots with thyme

White cabbage, leek and fennel cooked in garlicky white wine

Summer fruit Charlotte and clotted cream

Roast Pork with Crackling and Gingered Pears

1.3kg pork loin, boned and rolled
(please don't buy this in a
supermarket, go to your most
trusted butcher for a piece of
organic, happily-reared,
properly-scored pig)
salt and pepper, to taste
2 garlic cloves, peeled and crushed

3 teaspoons fennel seeds
2 tablespoons olive oil
3 pears
1 teaspoon ginger (fresh or from a
jar), grated
250ml white wine
2 teaspoons ready-made apple sauce

Bring the pork back to room temperature before you cook it. Preheat the oven to 220°C/Gas Mark 7. Dry the pork off with some kitchen towel and, if the fat hasn't already been scored by your butcher, take a Stanley knife and cut slits diagonally down the skin at intervals of 2cm or so. Anoint the skin liberally with salt (it should look like a carpet) and rub it in with the garlic and the fennel seeds. Put a roasting tin on the hob with the oil and brown the meaty sides of the joint. (As well as sealing in the juices, this should help the fat to crisp up.) Turn the pork skin-side up and slide the tin into the oven, turning the heat down to 200°C/Gas Mark 6 after 15–20 minutes. The pork will take 25 minutes per 500g and needs to rest for 10–15 minutes before carving.

While the pork is cooking, make the gingered pears. Take the pears, peel, quarter and core them and pop them in a pan with the grated fresh ginger (or the 'Lazy Ginger' that comes in a jar, made by the same people who make 'Lazy Chilli'. I know using this kind of stuff *is* lazy, but I am all for avoiding loathsome jobs. Every time I have tried to grate fresh ginger I end up grating my fingers as well). Add half of the white wine and let it all bubble away until the pears are soft and the juices are syrupy – for about

serves 6

5–10 minutes depending on how ripe your pears are. If you prefer, the pears can be prepared in advance and reheated until warm just before you are ready to serve the meat.

When the pork is cooked, remove it from the oven and put it on a plate. I didn't have time to do this as things were late enough as it was, but if your crackling needs a little perfecting, follow Nigella's advice: Remove the crackling from the joint and cut it into a few pieces – those that are crispy and those that are not. Any crackling that is smugly perfect can sit with the pork in a warm place, covered in foil, while it rests. (I usually put mine in the grill section of the oven, which is over my main oven. The grill's off, of course.) The soggier bits can go back into the oven on a baking tray, skin-side up, with the oven turned up again to 220°C/Gas Mark 7. Meanwhile, pour away any excess fat from the porky juices left in the roasting tin, add the rest of the wine and the apple sauce and simmer to allow the sauce to reduce. Test for seasoning, carve the pork, serve with the gingered pears, and 'pig' out.

Mustard Mash

1 kg floury maincrop potatoes, such
    as King Edwards or Maris Piper
2 tablespoons crème fraîche
4 tablespoons full-fat milk
about 50g butter

wholegrain mustard, to taste
    (I suggest 2 heaped teaspoons,
    but taste it to see if it needs
    more)

Peel the potatoes and cut them into medium-sized chunks. Put them in a large pan of well salted boiling water and cook for about 20–25 minutes or until soft. Meanwhile, heat the other ingredients together in another pan, or in a bowl in the microwave.

When the potatoes are ready, drain them well, wait until the steam dies down and add them to the other pan or bowl. Mash them into the artery-clogging buttery cream and beat it all together with an electric whisk. You can either do this so it's ready when you are ready to serve, or do it earlier and reheat it in the microwave or in a bowl over a pan of simmering water when you need it.

Roasted Carrots with Thyme

4 large carrots   **6 stalks of thyme**
knob of butter   **salt and pepper**

Scrub the carrots and slice them thickly in a diagonal fashion. Pop them in a pan of boiling water and parboil for 5 minutes. Meanwhile, put the butter and thyme leaves into a small roasting tin and slide it into the oven. When the butter has melted, remove, add the carrots, season well and toss everything together. Roast them below the pork for at least 45 minutes of its cooking time.

White Cabbage, Leek and Fennel Cooked in Garlicky White Wine

¹/₃ **of a white cabbage**
1 bulb of fennel
2 leeks, cleaned

120ml white wine
1 garlic clove, peeled and crushed
salt and pepper

Finely slice the white cabbage, fennel and the leeks. Pop the lot in a large pan with white wine and crushed garlic clove. Add some seasoning and let it cook down for about 10 minutes. That's it.

Summer Fruit Charlotte and Clotted Cream

This is a summer pudding for a British spring day. In fact, it's far nicer than genuine summer pudding, which I personally find a bit damp and soggy. Here, the bread adds a crispy contrast to the slushy summer fruits. I served it with clotted cream to give a nod towards real, sunny summer and the delights of cream teas. The father-in-law, ungrateful so-and-so that he is, said that, 'for his part' pouring cream would have been preferable. As the old blighter was already on his third portion by this point, his wife chastised him for his criticism and the Vicar merely begged to differ.

approx. 7 slices of white bread, cut about 1.5cm thick, crusts removed	150g blueberries
	150g blackberries
	3 tablespoons caster sugar, according to taste, plus extra for dusting (optional)
125g butter, 50g melted and the rest at room temperature	
250g raspberries	clotted cream, to serve

You'll need either an 850ml pudding basin or a soufflé dish.

Whilst I prepared the fruit, I got the men on to the bread bit. Before I could stop them they had sliced nearly a whole loaf – some of it extremely badly. However, they made up for it by coming up with the idea of only applying melted butter to one side of the bread and smearing the other 50g of the fresh stuff on the other. The bread has to line the dish, and they decided that freshly spread butter made an ideal glue to stick it to the sides. They were right.

serves 6

For the fruit: in a pan, lightly cook the berries with the sugar and the remaining 25g of softened butter over a medium heat for about 3–4 minutes. You want the fruit to soften very slightly but still retain its shape. Leave to cool if possible (I didn't have time).

Line the dish with about 5 slices of the buttery bread, overlapping them slightly and leaving no gaps, then pour in the fruit. Seal the top with the remaining bread by trimming and pushing it inside the edge of the upright bread; put a saucer on it and a bag of sugar, or something else quite heavy. After 30 minutes, take off the bag of sugar, leaving on the saucer, and put the dish in an oven preheated to 200°C/Gas Mark 6 for 30 minutes. After this time, remove the saucer with an oven glove and put the pudding back in for a final 5–10 minutes or until golden on top. Leave to rest for 10 minutes.

To serve, you could invert the pudding onto a plate if you want to look fancy, or serve it straight from the bowl or dish, cut into slices. Serve with cream (the pouring stuff, if John Beynon is a guest) and a little dusting of caster sugar, if you wish.

A spring lamb for friends

Some locals over today. It's the end of May – my favourite month of the year – and time for some lovely lamb and a Sunday lunch without the merest whiff of roast potatoes, vegetables and gravy. Much as I adore all that, come a dash of sun, a roast lamb dinner for friends needs to have a relaxed, Mediterranean or Middle Eastern twist. That means lots of herbs, lots of bright colours, and bags of flavour.

In this recipe the lamb is marinated overnight so that it is infused with a herby, lemony freshness that's set off by the warmth of cumin. The quinoa salad is a riot of colour, texture and taste, while the vegetables provide crunch and a salad, with its balsamic dressing, adds a touch of sweetness.

LEG OF LAMB WITH CUMIN, LEMON AND MINT

HOUMOUS DRESSING

ROASTED FENNEL AND LEEKS

TRAFFIC-LIGHT QUINOA

SPINACH SALAD

KING OF PUDDINGS

serves 4

Leg of Lamb with Cumin, Lemon and Mint

The meat needs to be at room temperature before it goes in the oven. For a churchgoer like me, this means taking the beast out of the fridge before I leave. I either put it somewhere safe, away from the cat, and do all the cooking bit when I get home; or I set the timer on my oven to come on when I'm out. With this lamb, I put it in after church time.

To be honest, I find the timing a bit tricky. In my oven, meat only takes the time cookery books tell you it will take if you sear it before it goes in, otherwise I have to add extra time. (Incidentally, I am a great believer in the whole searing thing. I know it seems nonsensical to stick the roast on the hob and brown it just before it's going to have a jolly old time in the oven, but it really does help it to get a fabulous crust and seal in the flavours.) However, what with the marinade and bits of mint sticking out everywhere, I chose not to do it on this occasion. It was all smelling pretty great and I was feeling quietly confident, smug even, as I took the lamb out of the oven at the end of its cooking time. I felt sure it would be perfection on legs – or on one, at least. However, as we cut it up, the middle of it was, quite frankly, raw. To avoid pure vampire-like blood consumption, those bits had to go back in the oven as seconds beckoned.

1 leg of lamb (mine was 1.15kg)
4 teaspoons cumin seeds, crushed
2 garlic cloves, peeled and crushed
3 tablespoons lemon oil

juice of $\frac{1}{2}$ lemon
1 tablespoon fresh mint, chopped
salt and pepper

On Saturday (or the day before, if you're not serving this on a Sunday), stab your lamb all over with the point of a small sharp knife. Mix the cumin seeds, garlic, lemon oil, lemon juice and mint together and rub it into the lamb. Season well with salt and pepper and pop the lovely leg into a carrier bag or something similar, then seal it and put it in the fridge.

The next day, take the lamb out of its carrier bag and put it in a roasting tin. For classic timings for roasting lamb (remember that ovens do vary), put it in an oven set to 230°C/Gas Mark 8. After 20 minutes, turn the heat down to 200°C/Gas Mark 6. After the initial 20 minute heat blast, the meat should take 15 minutes per 500g. For rare meat cook for 12 minutes per 500g; 25 minutes per 500g for well done. When it comes out of the oven at the end of the cooking time, the meat needs to rest somewhere warm, covered with foil, for 10–20 minutes.

Serve the lamb cut into slices and with the houmous dressing, the quinoa, roasted fennel and leeks on the side. Tell your guests to smear the houmous dressing over their meat at will. Add a sunny day, some lovely people and, in our case, a roof terrace, and you can't really beat it.

Houmous Dressing

5 big tablespoons houmous,
   preferably homemade
   (see page 213)
3 tablespoons olive oil

1 tablespoon lemon juice (optional)
black pepper
2 small handfuls of pine nuts

For the houmous dressing, mix the houmous with the oil, more lemon if you want a bit more zing, and a bit more black pepper. Pour into a flattish bowl. Toast the pine nuts in a dry frying pan and don't take your eyes off them – you know it's true: look away for one second and they'll burn. Scatter them over the dressing and let people help themselves.

Roasted Fennel and Leeks

I know, I know, it's fennel and leeks together again; it's just that I don't think either of them get used enough and I am on a campaign to get them noticed!

4 leeks, thoroughly cleaned

1 bulb of fennel

3 tablespoons olive oil

juice of $\frac{1}{2}$ lemon

2 teaspoons coriander seeds, crushed

salt and pepper

The leeks need to be chopped into 2cm chunks and the fennel sliced lengthways into about 8 wedges. Cut off some of the fennel's core, but leave just enough to keep each wedge together. Put the vegetables in a roasting tray and mix in the olive oil, lemon juice and crushed coriander seeds, along with lots of salt and pepper. They can go in the oven under the lamb and will take about 40 minutes at 200°C/Gas Mark 6. Give them a stir a couple of times during the cooking time.

serves 4

Traffic-light Quinoa

First, quinoa is pronounced 'keen–wah', and second, it's lovely, as well as healthy. (Just don't drop an opened bag of the stuff on the floor unless you want your kitchen to look like a beach.) If you can't find quinoa, you could use couscous or bulgar wheat.

enough quinoa to come up to the 250ml mark in a measuring jug (approx. 250g)
500ml cold water
2 peppers – one red, one yellow
6 tablespoons olive oil
2 tablespoons lemon juice
4 cherry or baby plum tomatoes, quartered

4 spring onions, trimmed and chopped
1 forefinger's length of cucumber, cut into small dice
200g feta – partly crumbled, partly cubed
large bunch of fresh basil, torn
salt and pepper

Rinse the quinoa in a sieve then put it in a pan with the cold water. It needs to come to the boil and then simmer away for 15–20 minutes or until the water is absorbed and it is soft and fluffy. Meanwhile, preheat the grill to high.

De-seed and halve the peppers and pop them under a hot grill, skin-side up, until the skins are black and charred. Once they are ready, remove and wait a bit before pulling the skins off. (I never can be bothered and end up nearly burning my fingers off.) Cut the peppers into thin strips – it's easiest to use kitchen scissors for this, as de-skinned peppers are slippery little things. Once the quinoa is done, tip it into a serving bowl and add all the other ingredients. Stir to combine and leave it on the side until you are about to eat.

Spinach Salad

about 400g baby spinach leaves

For the dressing:
3 tablespoons olive oil

1 tablespoon balsamic vinegar
1 teaspoon French mustard
1 garlic clove, peeled and crushed
salt and pepper, to taste

You don't need me to tell you to put the spinach leaves in a bowl, combine the ingredients for the dressing and toss them both together. Oops, I just did.

This menu didn't feature a heavy main course, so for pudding I beefed things up just a little. Here, I give you my version of the old-fashioned dessert, 'Queen of Puddings'. Mine, made with mellow apricot jam, is less oh-so-sweet and has a kind of hidden depth. Like some men. So, my version got a gender change.

575ml full-fat milk	finely grated zest of 1 lemon or
40g butter	orange
150g fresh white breadcrumbs	4 generous tablespoons good-
2 tablespoons ground almonds	quality apricot jam
150g caster sugar	4 large eggs

You can make this in an oval pie dish or a big shallow ovenproof bowl. It should be around 1.2–1.5 litres in capacity.

Bring the milk to the boil in a pan. Once it's boiling, take it off the heat and stir in the butter, breadcrumbs, the ground almonds, 25g of the sugar and the zest of whichever fruit you have opted for. Leave on the side for ½ hour to allow the bread to swell and the flavours to combine.

After that time, melt the jam and pour half of it over the base of the dish and preheat the oven to 180°C/Gas Mark 4. Separate the eggs: put the egg whites into a large, clean mixing bowl and the yolks into a cup. Beat the yolks briefly with a fork and add them to the breadcrumb mixture. Pour this over the jam and bake in the oven for around 25–30 minutes until softly set.

Meanwhile, whisk together the egg whites until they form soft peaks and then gradually whisk in the remaining 125g of sugar until stiff. When the pudding comes out of the oven, pour over the remaining warm jam, spreading it to cover all the breadcrumb mixture. Pile over the meringue and swirl it out with the back of a spoon to make a seal with the edge of the dish. Put the dish back in the oven for around 10 minutes or until the meringue is golden.

A whole salmon, preferably eaten in the sun

My baby cousin and her husband are staying. Blonde and tiny, I can't believe
she's now a grown-up, married woman. Yesterday they took us out for a lovely
lunch. Today, it's my turn to cook and I want to give them a treat. The air is
soft and muggy, so I have plumped for lunch in the garden and a whole
salmon. I'd bought some oysters to kick things off and my cousin and I
enjoyed the performance as the men vied with each other in a manly display
of oyster-opening prowess. You don't have to have oysters if you don't want
them (especially if you are of the opinion that they taste of salty snot!) but for
me they were just what we needed before the delicate creaminess of what was
to come.

Salmon is quite a rich fish, so an invigorating slap in the face beforehand, in
the form of oysters, set me up to appreciate its flavour. As for the pudding;
it's just as rich, but somehow it doesn't seem so. Heady with oranges, it
retains its lightness and the only thing in it that's likely to make you want to
nod off is the generous quantity of Cointreau.

SALMON STUFFED WITH HERBS AND GARLIC

ROASTED BABY POTATOES

GREEN SALAD WITH BROAD BEANS AND GOAT'S CHEESE

PANETTONE TRIFLE

Salmon Stuffed with Herbs and Garlic

4 spring onions, trimmed and finely
   chopped
4 garlic cloves, peeled and crushed
25g, flatleaf parsley, chopped
1¹⁄₂ tablespoons tarragon, chopped
1 tablespoon olive oil
salt and pepper

1 whole salmon (about 2kg)
big handful of dill, chopped
200ml soured cream
1 large bunch of asparagus, trimmed
knob of butter (optional)
3 lemons

Preheat the oven to 160°C/Gas Mark 3. Combine the spring onions, garlic, parsley, tarragon and oil in a bowl and season well. Place the fish on a large piece of foil that has been lightly brushed with oil and stuff the cavity with the spring onion and herb mixture. Wrap the fish up in the foil and pleat the edges together to make a good seal. Place the fish parcel on a large baking tray so that the foil pleat is at the top when it goes in the oven. Put it in the oven: if the salmon is over 2.5kg, cook for 10 minutes per 450g and add 10 minutes to the cooking time; if it weighs less than that, cook for 15 minutes per 450g, then add 15 minutes. In my oven it took 1 hour and 10 minutes to reach lightly cooked perfection.

If I were you, I'd open the top of the foil and start sticking a knife in the middle as the cooking time reaches its final stages. The flesh should be opaque but still moist, and the fish should come away from the bones easily. It'd be a shame to have spent good money on a beautiful fresh salmon for it to end up overcooked and only fit to feed people at wedding receptions. (Some wedding caterers seem to be able to squeeze moistness out of a salmon with the skill that house-proud types wring out their dishcloths.)

serves 6

Next, mix the dill with the soured cream and add lots of salt and pepper. This potion is to be smeared on the salmon and potatoes alike whilst you are eating.

Shortly before the salmon is ready, cook the asparagus. You can either boil it in salted water or steam it, but either way it should take about 3–5 minutes. Drain and toss with some salt and pepper and maybe a small knob of butter.

Once the salmon is ready, remove it from the foil parcel and put it on a big serving plate. If you have fiddled a lot with it to test if it's ready whilst it was in the oven, remove the skin and make sure the other side is facing upwards, otherwise people will think a cat's been at it. Remove the rest of the skin and the head, if seeing them would put your guests off their food. Squeeze the juice of 1 lemon over the fish and cut the other 2 into quarters. Arrange the asparagus around and over the fish, along with the lemon quarters. Serve the salmon with the salad, roasted baby potatoes and creamy dill sauce. The eating of it reduced four people with chatty Welsh blood in their veins to silence. Well, almost.

Roasted Baby Potatoes

500g baby new potatoes
3 tablespoons olive oil
salt and pepper

Whilst the salmon is cooking, wash the potatoes, or scrape them, if you prefer. I am lucky in that I have two ovens, so I cooked them in a small roasting tin, bathed in olive oil, at 200°C/Gas Mark 6 for 1 hour. If you haven't got two ovens, then just serve boiled potatoes, cooked for 20–25 minutes or until just tender. When they are ready, they need an abundance of salt and pepper.

Green Salad with Broad Beans and Goat's Cheese

The Vicar would never choose to eat broad beans, so I sneak them into his summer meals as subtly as I can. For me, they ooze nostalgia, conjuring up happily shared conspiracies with my long-gone father. He would pick them from the garden, my mother would cook them, and then he and I would eat a big plate full of them, all by themselves, secretly slathering them in butter when my mother wasn't looking.

3 tablespoons olive oil
1 tablespoon balsamic vinegar
a pinch of mustard powder
salt and pepper
2 handfuls of broad beans

600g green leaves (I used baby spinach, rocket and watercress)
50g Chèvre cheese, crumbled into small chunks

First, combine the oil, vinegar, mustard powder and seasoning together in a small bowl. Next, cook the beans in boiling salted water for 1–2 minutes or until tender, then drain them, tip them into a serving bowl and add the dressing while they are still hot. Leave them like this until you are ready to serve. Add the salad leaves and Chèvre and toss together well.

Panettone Trifle

This is a make-ahead dessert. If you are planning on eating it for lunch you could still prepare it in the morning, but it would make your day more relaxed if you don't. I made mine the afternoon before, when I had a rare moment of kitchen quiet.

5 slices of panettone, cut about 1.5 cm thick

6 tablespoons Cointreau

2 large tablespoons good-quality marmalade (I bought breakfast marmalade from my butcher but thick-cut, quality marmalade is fine – something like Frank Cooper's)

3 oranges

5 fresh apricots

1 tablespoon apricot jam

1 tablespoon water

75g caster sugar, plus 1 tablespoon

250ml full-fat milk

500ml double cream

6 egg yolks

seeds from 1 vanilla pod, or a few drops of vanilla extract

1 teaspoon cornflour

1 tablespoon flaked almonds, lightly toasted

First, break up the slices of panettone and put them into a 1.5-litre serving bowl. Slosh on the booze, then put the marmalade in a small pan, warm gently and pour that over the panettone, too. Finely grate the zest of 1 of the oranges and put it in a bowl. Shave off the zest from the remaining 2 oranges with a potato peeler, cover, and set aside for decoration. Now take a thin slice off the top and bottom of each orange, sit them one at a time on a chopping board and carefully slice away all the skin and white pith – which is one of those jobs that everybody hates.

Then slice away the segments from between the pieces of membrane and cut each one in half. Put the apricots into a small pan with the jam, water and the 1 tablespoon of sugar and poach gently for 10 minutes or until just tender, then mix into the finely grated zest with the orange pieces. Pour the whole lot over the Cointreau-sloshed panettone base.

Now for the custard. As a child I hated two things: custard and boys. The first, because it was too sloppy; the second, because they weren't sloppy enough (that is, for all non-Welsh readers, they weren't much into kissing and the like). Anyway, I love both now, so custard here we come. In a large pan, heat up the milk and 300ml of the cream. Meanwhile, whisk together the egg yolks, vanilla seeds or extract, the sugar and cornflour in a big bowl. Once the milky cream is hot, add it gradually to the egg mixture, whisking all the time. Pour it back into the pan, the heat turned to low, and stir constantly until it has thickened enough to coat the back of a spoon. Pour it through a sieve on top of the fruity stuff already in your serving bowl. Cover and let it cool for a few hours or overnight in the fridge.

When you are ready to serve, whip up the rest of the double cream and smear it over the top of the custard. Once you have sprinkled over the almonds and pieces of reserved orange zest, it's at last time to dig in.

A different sort of Sunday

I have to confess that I do like a big slab of meat on my plate on a Sunday, but there is no reason not to play the wild card now and then. Here, I offer a showcase for crab; in this recipe its delicate freshness is offset by the rich fruitiness of the tomato and the indulgent creamy sauces.

The pudding is equally a picture of elegance: passion fruit may look ugly when uncut, but once opened it releases a mound of tiny, glinting, flavour-packed jewels, with a heady fragrance.

FRESH CRAB CANNELLONI

PAVLOVAS WITH PASSION FRUIT CURD AND CREAM

Fresh Crab Cannelloni

A cheap and cheerful version of this, which is more suitable for a simple midweek supper, could be to replace the crabmeat with tinned tuna or salmon. A dish the children will love …

200g fresh white crabmeat
juice of ¹/₂ lemon
3 teaspoons lemon-infused olive oil
a pinch of cayenne pepper
salt and pepper
a handful of fresh basil leaves,
    shredded
250g fresh egg lasagne sheets

For the tomato sauce:
2 tablespoons olive oil
1 medium onion, peeled and finely
    chopped
2 garlic cloves, peeled and crushed
1 x 400g tin chopped tomatoes
2 teaspoons caster or granulated
    sugar
juice of ¹/₂ lemon
salt and pepper

For the cheese sauce:
1 onion, peeled and halved
6 cloves
900ml full-fat milk
2 bay leaves
1 teaspoon black peppercorns
60g butter
60g plain flour
4 tablespoons double cream
120g finely grated Parmesan or
    Cheddar cheese, plus 30g
    Parmesan to sprinkle on the top
2 egg yolks
salt and pepper

For the cheese sauce, stud the onion with the cloves and put it in a pan with the milk, bay leaves and black peppercorns. Bring the milk to the boil, take the pan off the heat and set aside for 20 minutes to allow the flavours to infuse.

Meanwhile, get cracking on the tomato sauce. Heat the oil in a medium-sized pan and add the onion. Cook for a few minutes until softened then add the garlic and cook for 5 minutes more, taking care the contents of the pan don't brown. Add the tomatoes and sugar and simmer gently for 15–20 minutes, stirring now and then, until reduced and thickened. Squeeze in the lemon juice, add some salt and pepper and spoon the sauce over the base of a rectangular, ovenproof dish (around 30cm x 20cm and 5cm deep) in which the cannelloni will fit side by side in two parallel rows.

For the cannelloni filling, mix the crabmeat together with the lemon juice, lemon oil, cayenne pepper and salt and pepper. Finally, stir through the basil.

Bring a large pan of salted water to the boil. Drop in the sheets of lasagne one at a time and leave in there for 5 minutes. (I know fresh pasta is supposed to be 'ready-to-roll', as it were, but it can often be a bit stiff. Here, you want to be sure the sheets are floppy and pliable, especially as they are encasing the deliciously delicate crab.) Drain the pasta well, place the sheets side by side on a large piece of clingfilm and leave to cool. Spoon some of the crab filling along one short edge of each sheet and roll up. Arrange the cannelloni seam-side down on top of the tomato sauce. Preheat the oven to 200°C/Gas Mark 6. Bring the milk back to the boil, then strain it into a jug. Melt the butter in a pan, add the flour and cook over a medium heat for 1 minute. Gradually beat in the milk and bring it to the boil, stirring, then leave to simmer very gently over a low heat for 5 minutes, giving it a stir every now and then. Remove the pan from the heat and stir in the cream, 120g of the cheese, the egg yolks and salt and pepper to taste. Pour the cheese sauce over the cannelloni, sprinkle over the rest of the cheese and bake for 30 minutes until golden. Serve with a salad and maybe some bread.

Mini Pavlovas with Passion Fruit Curd and Cream

The trick to choosing good passion fruit is to select those that are really wrinkly (sometimes looks can be deceptive), as these will yield the most juice and the sweetest pulp.

Serves six, but four people may find it more than easy to polish them off.

3 egg whites
a very small pinch of salt
175g caster sugar
1 teaspoon cornflour
$^1/_2$ teaspoon white wine vinegar

For the topping:
300ml double cream
6 tablespoons passion fruit curd (or lemon, if you can't get it)
6 large passion fruit

Preheat the oven to 140°C/Gas Mark 1. Lightly grease a large baking tray and line with a sheet of non-stick baking paper.

Put the egg whites into a large, dry mixing bowl, add the salt and whisk with a hand-held electric mixer until the eggs form stiff peaks. Whisk in the sugar, 1 tablespoon at a time, to make a very stiff, glossy meringue. Whisk in the cornflour and vinegar.

Drop 6 even-sized spoonfuls of the mixture onto the prepared baking sheet, well spaced apart, and flatten them slightly with the back of the spoon, making a small dip in the centre. Bake for 45 minutes then turn off the oven and leave them inside to go cold – this will stop them cracking and collapsing.

Just before serving, whip the cream in a bowl into soft peaks and cut the passion fruits in half. Randomly spoon the curd over the whipped cream in the bowl and, as you spoon it out on top of each pavlova, swirl together briefly. Finish each pavlova with a scoop of passion fruit pulp and scoff.

Autumn and winter

Sunday lunch during the colder months means one thing to me: comfort. The sweet waft of parsnips roasting in the oven, the burnished, crunchy skins of the roast potatoes, and the wine-infused gravy bubbling away on the stove all calm and reassure and make me feel half-ready to face whatever a freezing Monday morning in January might throw at me. Most wonderfully, the cold months bring forth the perfect vegetables to wrap us up in warmth: just as our longing for salady lightness evaporates, we are provided with the likes of celeriac to mash with cream and potatoes, squashes to roast and various cabbages to provide a healthy punch of hot nutrition. And then, of course, there are all those gloriously homely winter puddings to think of …

A simple Sunday

These recipes are intended for two: a tired two. Perhaps two people who are a little jaded; maybe feeling a bit sick of the Christmas and New Year party overload; who want – no, need – clean, restorative, health-giving, but undemanding, food. However, this could also serve four – just double up the veg and the pudding.

The chicken dish is the sort of food that medieval toothless peasants might have had bubbling away regularly over their fires but that we, with our over-developed taste for reductions and contrast of flavours, and, well, our many teeth, hardly ever eat. Which is a shame really, as this dish is good for all kinds of reasons: not only is it healthy, but it also requires very little labour – if you want, you can stagger out of bed at any hour you please, assemble it, pop it on the lowest heat and go back to bed until next Christmas. Not only that, but the leftovers provide two more meals for the two of you, which, in a month that brings both a longing for rest and a desire to tighten the belt (both physically as well as financially), is probably just what you are after.

Finishing off the meal, the baked apples offer a way of using up the Christmas mincemeat in a way that will neither break the bank nor bring on the bloat.

January chicken

Stir-fried pak choi with sesame seeds

Mincemeat-stuffed baked apples

January Chicken

NOTE: You will require a big, cauldron-like pan to make this. You may think you don't need one but, believe me, you do; especially if you really like cooking but hate all the sloshing about that occurs when you haven't got a big enough pan. I have two such cauldrons: one medium and one massive, which seems to be designed for a tall witch with really strong arms. I used the medium-sized one for this chicken recipe.

1 small organic or free-range chicken (mine was 1.5kg)

2 medium onions, peeled and quartered

4 garlic cloves, peeled and crushed

3 medium carrots, peeled and chopped into 2cm chunks

2 leeks, cleaned and chopped into 2cm chunks

1 litre water

3 bay leaves

$\frac{1}{2}$ lemon

4 teaspoons sweet white miso paste

salt and pepper

Put all the ingredients, bar the miso paste, in your 'witching' pan. Without the option of a lie-in – it being a church day – I put my brew on the lowest setting on the top of the stove. It went on at 9.30am and then I dashed out of the door, worrying I would spend the whole of the sermon praying against a house fire. Anyway, all was well. I got home at 12 and the chicken was still not fully cooked. So I turned up the heat for 30 minutes, adding the miso at this point and testing for seasoning. I had to turn it down to its lowest heat again when the phone rang, but nothing spoilt. We ate at about one o'clock.

serves 2

Basically, this is a dish that could never, in a million years, be accused of being sophisticated (it's about as sophisticated as drinking warm milk at Grandma's kitchen table), but sometimes that's exactly where you want to be. Anyway, I removed the bird from the cauldron, chopped off the legs and served them on a base of half of the stocky slush (made during the cooking of the chicken, water and vegetables), with some pak choi on the side. For the Vicar, this last bit was a healthy step too far.

Here are some thrifty ideas for using up the leftovers:

chicken soup

Pull the rest of the meat off the carcass and add to the remainder of the vegetables and liquid left in the pan. Reheat and blitz in a food processor or liquidiser, or use a hand-held number until it is soupy. If the result is too thick, add some boiling water to thin it down a bit. What you'll get is a softly spoken soup that serves two, with seconds.

light and lazy stock

I nearly didn't bother making a stock from the bones of this bird; after all, it had already been sitting in liquid, bubbling away, for 3 hours. But I did decide to do it after all, but to make it simple. So I half-heartedly chucked the carcass in the pan, didn't bother with vegetables, nor bay leaves, filled up the big pan it was in with 2 litres of water and let it come to the boil and then simmer for a few hours. It was worth it: it wasn't the richest of stocks, but it was still good enough to use in another light broth or a risotto. I was left feeling like a virtuously thrifty wartime housewife. My grandmother would have been proud.

serves 2

Stir-fried Pak Choi with Sesame Seeds

1 tablespoon sesame or groundnut oil
1 head of pak choi

1 garlic clove, peeled and crushed
1 tablespoon sesame seeds, lightly toasted in a dry frying pan

Heat the oil in a wok, or similar, and chop the pak choi into slices. Throw it into the smoking pan with the garlic and toss for 3–4 minutes. Serve with the sesame seeds sprinkled haphazardly over the top.

Mincemeat-stuffed Baked Apples

Plan the cooking of these apples so that they can be served straight away, as they will collapse if they are left to stand. Old-fashioned this pudding may well be, but sometimes the old ways are the very best.

2 Bramley apples

For the mincemeat filling:
4 tablespoons good-quality mincemeat
20g toasted hazelnuts, coarsely chopped

20g dried cranberries or 20g ready-to-eat apricots, chopped
finely grated zest of $\frac{1}{2}$ orange
2 teaspoons brandy (optional)

custard or single cream, to serve (optional)

First, make the mincemeat filling by mixing all the ingredients together in a bowl. Preheat the oven to 200°C/Gas Mark 6.

Core the apples with an apple corer and then open up the cavity a little more with a swivel potato peeler, making sure that the resulting hole is at least 2.5–3cm across so that there is plenty of room for the filling. Then score a horizontal line around the centre of each one, just through the skin, to prevent them bursting whilst they're in the oven. Place the apples in a shallow, lightly buttered ovenproof dish. Generously fill the centre of each one with the mincemeat mixture. Pour 6 tablespoons of water into the bottom of the dish, cover it loosely with foil and bake for 30 minutes. After this time, remove the foil and bake for a further 15–20 minutes or until the apples are soft and tender right through to the centre.

Serve straight away with the syrupy juices and lashings of custard.

Bargain-basement lunch

You don't have to be penny-pinching to cook this, but if you are, it will only add to your enjoyment of it. This lunch gives you comfort food to be proud of; so cheap to make that you'll want to tell all your budget-minded, bargain-hunting friends about it.

All too easily we overlook the cheaper cuts of meat, nervous that, unlike our wartime predecessors, we don't know what to do with them. However, we ignore these cuts to our loss as, even for the most incompetent cook, they are a breeze to get the best out of and will save us money to buy new shoes.

We didn't actually have this for lunch on the day we cooked it because we had to go to a child's birthday bash after church. Instead, we had it with family members in the evening, bowls on knees, eyes glued to the rugby (the boys) while chatting aimlessly (the girls). It all felt wonderfully relaxed and cosy. On a chilly Sunday this would make a really fabulous lunch. Ideally, you would prepare it the day before and gently reheat it when you want to eat it. Or, if that's not possible, cook it on the day, stick it in the oven, go out in the fresh air and come back to a feast full of cheaply gained flavour.

BEEF STEW

RAREBIT TOASTS

LEMON RICE PUDDING

Beef Stew

2 tablespoons plain flour
salt and pepper
850g brisket of beef, cut into 2.5cm
    chunks
2 tablespoons olive oil
6 small, or 3 large, carrots, cut into
    2cm chunks
3 parsnips, quartered, cores removed
    and cut into 2cm chunks

2 onions, peeled and thickly sliced
3 celery sticks, thinly sliced
500ml Guinness
6 sprigs of thyme
1 x 400g tin plum tomatoes
8 pickled walnuts (that's a jar's
    worth)
2–3 teaspoons Worcestershire sauce

Preheat the oven to 160°C/Gas Mark 3. Put the flour into a bowl, add salt and pepper and toss in the pieces of brisket. Now heat the oil in a large, flameproof casserole dish on the top of the stove and throw in the beef, in batches if necessary, to brown off the pieces. You'll need to be on hand to stir things round, as the meat may stick. Return the meat to the pan, add all the vegetables and then the rest of the ingredients. Let it all come to the boil, put the lid on the casserole and put it in the oven.

Leave it in there for 2½ hours or until the meat is tender. If the juices look too liquidy when you take it out of the oven, you can put the casserole on a high heat on the hob and let the stew bubble away, uncovered, for a few minutes. Test for seasoning, then serve in bowls with the rarebit toasts floating on top.

serves 4

Rarebit Toasts

These aren't real rarebits, but rather something far simpler. But they do the trick.

4 tablespoons grated cheese
    (Cheddar, Lancashire or
    Wensleydale)
2 teaspoons wholegrain mustard

1 egg, beaten
4 thick slices of good-quality bread
    (white or brown is fine)

Preheat the grill to high a few minutes before you are ready to eat. Mix the cheese, mustard and beaten egg together in a bowl. Put the slices of bread onto the rack of the grill pan and toast on both sides. Remove and spread each one with some of the cheesy egg mixture. Put the toasts back under the grill until bubbling and brown in places. Cut the toasts in half and float them on top of the stew.

serves 4

Lemon Rice Pudding

When I was a child, Sunday lunch always meant rice pudding, so I connect it with sitting in a warm kitchen, feeling snug and cared for. Rice pudding is the opposite of flashy, 'Look at me, aren't I gorgeous?' food: it merely exists to soothe. I added some good lemon curd to mine. My guests said it tasted very special and had I gone to lots of effort? My response, in one word, was, 'No'.

75g short-grain pudding rice
600ml full-fat milk
150ml single cream (naughty, I
    know, but just use all milk if you
    want to lower the fat content)

2 tablespoons caster sugar
finely grated zest of 2 lemons
6 tablespoons lemon curd
    (homemade or good-quality
    bought stuff)

Put the rice, milk, cream, sugar and lemon zest into a 1.2 litre shallow ovenproof dish and put it in the oven at 150°C/Gas Mark 2 for 1¼ hours, stirring in the skin every 30 minutes. When you remove it from the oven it won't look very thick. Stir in the lemon curd and it will miraculously thicken, with a little more sugar to taste if you wish. If there's any left, which I very much doubt, it would also be rather nice cold.

serves 4

Tradition with a twist

Given a topside of beef my intention is to go down the traditional route with Yorkshire pudding and the works. However, on one occasion I ran short on time and so we had to make do without the puds. We ended up staying at the table long after the children had left it to go elsewhere to play, while my brother-in-law shared with us his dad's favourite way of ensuring perfect potatoes. Apparently, Daddy Mackenzie would parboil them at coffee time; drain them; distress them lightly and then pop them in boiling hot fat in a roasting tray in the oven. And then – and here's the surprising bit – he'd take them out again, leave them on the side to cool down in the fat and then put them back in the oven for 45 minutes as lunchtime approached. The brother-in-law said this embossed the potatoes with a gooey, toffee-like colour and sweetness. Maybe we should all give the 'Mackenzie Method' a try and compare notes.

ROAST BEEF

THE ROAST POTATOES

CARROT AND CUMIN PURÉE

TWO CABBAGES WITH APPLE AND RED ONION

TOFFEE AND APPLE CRUMBLE

Roast Beef

1.2kg topside of beef
1 teaspoon mustard powder
salt and pepper
3 tablespoons olive oil

For the gravy:
the meat juices

1 tablespoon flour
120ml red wine
350ml beef stock (fresh, or made
    from a good-quality liquid
    bouillon)
salt and pepper

I didn't muck about much with the beef. I just rubbed the mustard powder over the outside of the joint and seasoned it. Then I poured the oil into a roasting tin, heated it on the hob and seared the beef in the hot fat until it was nicely browned all over. It then went in a hot oven preheated to 250°C/Gas Mark 9 for 15 minutes. After that I turned it down to 180°C/Gas Mark 4, cooking it for 18 minutes per 500g. At the end of the cooking time I took it out of the oven and left it in a warm place, covered in foil, to give it a good rest. It was brown at the ends (so suitable for the children) and pink to red in the middle (perfect for us adults).

Whilst the meat was resting, I made the gravy. To be honest, I find it difficult to give a recipe for this as I kind of feel my way in gravy-making; I believe that making gravy is a great way to learn how to cook instinctively. If you are nervous about making it on the stove right before you are ready to serve and while guests may well be hovering, take the meat out of its baking tray 20 minutes or so before the end of its cooking time, and return it to the oven in a clean tray, as most of the meat juices and stickiness will already be in the original tin. Get on with making the gravy using the roasting tin of juices.

How you make your gravy is up to you: you could just add some wine to the meat juices to make a little *jus* (don't you just hate that word?), but I opted to go down a more old-fashioned route: in other words, I used flour. If this is how you want to do it, remove the meat from the original tin (to rest or to return to the oven) and put this tin, containing all the meat juices, on the hob and stir in the plain flour (it will look a bit gluey when you do this). Add the red wine, stirring constantly, and then the beef stock. (I used a beef liquid bouillon mixed with the cooking water from the vegetables.) Add salt and pepper and let it bubble away and reduce. Keep tasting it and add more stock or wine, if you think it needs it. When it is ready, pour it in a pan, ready to serve or reheat later. If you are making it a little in advance, add any extra meat juices from the new baking tin when you reheat the gravy.

I am a bit obsessive about gravy and constantly fret there won't be enough, so when people go for seconds I am there, bossily waving the gravy boat in their faces, lest they forget to anoint their fresh portion with my lovingly made sauce.

The Roast Potatoes

Again, I don't think one really needs a recipe for this as everyone seems to have their own tips and tricks for how to make the perfect roastie. (See the 'Mackenzie Method' on page 54.) Here are my personal hints.

1.5kg floury maincrop potatoes, such as King Edwards or Maris Piper

2 tablespoons goose fat or lard
salt

Peel the potatoes and cut them into medium-sized pieces. (I tend to go for a sort of triangle shape as I cut them up.) Put them in a pan of salted boiling water and pop on a lid. Parboil them for 10 minutes or so, then pour them into a colander. Put the lid from the pan on top of the colander and hold it down as you give the potatoes a really good shake. (I do this shaking business in the colander rather than the pan as a heavy pan full of potatoes is a bit too cumbersome for me to handle.)

Preheat the oven to 210°C/Gas Mark 7. Put the fat into a roasting tin and put in the oven to heat up. Once it has melted, remove the tin from the oven and put it on the hob over a medium heat. Now introduce the potatoes to the fat and turn the potatoes in it until they are all evenly coated. Do be careful as you do this because the fat may well spit at you. Put the potatoes in the oven. (Ideally you should cook them in a separate oven from the beef, but if you haven't got one, compromise by cooking the beef at 200°C/Gas Mark 6 and whack up the heat once the beef comes out.)

Most cookery books say that roast potatoes take around 50 minutes, but I have found that they usually take longer than that – about 1–1¼ hours. You want them fluffy inside and looking like they do in the Mackenzie household. Remove from the oven, sprinkle with a good amount of salt and serve.

Carrot and Cumin Purée

Making this reminds me of the endless purée-making I did for my children when I was weaning them. However, this concoction, with its creamy cumin headiness, is a far more adult affair. It would also be delicious served to liven up a chicken breast cooked with lemon and garlic or a plainly cooked lamb chop.

750g carrots, peeled and chopped into 5cm lengths
100ml cream (single or double)

2 teaspoons ground cumin (or maybe more, depending on your taste)
salt and pepper

Put the carrots in boiling salted water and boil for 7–8 minutes until soft. Drain off the water (reserving it for the gravy or making soup), pour in the cream and stir in the cumin and some seasoning. Blend the whole lot together using a hand-held blender or a food processor and reheat, if necessary, before serving.

an alternative purée
Parsnip and swede also make a fine purée, and making it is a sneaky way of getting people who claim to hate swede to eat it.

Peel 5 parsnips, chop them into chunks and do the same with half of a small swede or a quarter of a large one. Boil in salted water until soft – about 20–25 minutes – and drain, saving the cooking water. Pour 100ml of milk and 100ml of cream into the pan you used to cook the vegetables, and heat it up. Add the parsnips and swede, mash together and whisk with an electric whisk. Add salt and pepper, a knob of butter and maybe some freshly grated nutmeg.

serves 6

Two Cabbages with Apple and Red Onion

One of the reasons I love my weekly organic vegetable box is that it forces me, and those who eat with me, to partake of food I could easily avoid or overlook. Take the cabbage family: so often the cabbage conjures up memories of bad smells and soggy school dinners, and so we can be inclined to give anything related to it a wide berth. However, cooked with a light touch, cabbage and suchlike can be wonderful. One day, with a red cabbage and a small green one asking to be eaten, I knocked up the following as a side dish to the beef.

$^1/_2$ **red cabbage, de-cored and cut into chunks**
1 apple (I used a Cox's), quartered and cored
1 red onion
2 tablespoons olive oil

1 garlic clove, peeled and crushed
2 tablespoons white wine
1 green cabbage, de-cored
knob of butter
salt and pepper

First, get out your food processor and find your slicing disc. Use it to cut up the red cabbage, the apple and the onion. (You could use the other half of the cabbage to make the red cabbage and Stilton slaw on page 263.) Put the oil in a large pan and add the red cabbage, onion, apple and garlic. Put a lid on the pan and make sure the heat is at medium. Give it all a stir from time to time and let it cook for about 15 minutes, or until the cabbage has softened but still has some crunch. Then pour in the wine and let it bubble away.

Meanwhile, finely shred the green cabbage and add it to the pan, stirring until it is wilting nicely, which should only take a few minutes. Add a knob of butter and season.

Toffee and Apple Crumble

If the title of this dessert conjures up a picture of funfair toffee apples, I do apologise. Banish those thoughts of toothache-inducing candied fruit on sticks and instead think of sticky, caramel sweetness (oh dear, that's all a bit confusingly redolent of Mackenzie parsnips). This pudding produced lively remembrances of crumbles from the past. My husband's sister talked lovingly about her mother's thick crumble toppings. 'Goodness, you are just so toppist!' exclaimed the brother-in-law. 'Fine,' came the reply, 'you can have my bottom and I'll have your top.' An interesting prospect …

1kg Cox's apples, peeled, quartered and cored
juice of 1 lemon
8-10 tablespoons ready-made toffee sauce (this is almost a 220g jar)
225g plain flour
175g chilled butter, cut into small pieces
pinch of salt
50g porridge oats
150g demerara sugar

You will need a 2-litre ovenproof dish. I mistakenly used one with ridges on the bottom – don't: all the lovely caramel sinks into the cracks and has to be scraped out laboriously.

Preheat the oven to 190°C/Gas Mark 5. Slice each apple quarter into 4, place in a bowl, stir in the toffee sauce and lemon juice and then spoon evenly over the base of the dish.

serves 6

Now take out your food processor and throw in the flour, butter and salt and blitz until the butter is mixed in and the mixture looks like rough breadcrumbs. Stir in the oats and sugar and work the mixture with your fingers a little until it starts to stick together in little clumps. Sprinkle the mixture on top of the apples. Cook in the oven for 40–45 minutes until golden and bubbling, and serve with cream or ice cream.

A celebration of old traditions and new friends

It's late November and my son has already been talking about Christmas for weeks. On a dark and rainy Sunday I opt to give in to his excitement and serve a lunch with more than a sniff of festive tradition about it. Some newly acquired friends are with us and, as we finish our meal and share unusual moments from our pasts, the lovely Helen calmly relates one of her own memories: 'I once fired an AK47 in the desert at a cactus. I was on a holiday with an ex-con. Later, I stroked a tarantula. After that, my friend broke his leg and we went skiing.' As far as surreal anecdotes go, we couldn't really top that and rapidly moved on to coffee.

DUCK LEGS WITH PORT AND CRANBERRIES

CELERIAC AND POTATO GRATIN OR MASH

TURNIPS AND LEEKS WITH HONEY, CORIANDER AND SOY

WILTED SPINACH

WINTER FRUIT PIE

serves 6

Duck Legs with Port and Cranberries

I assembled this dish the evening before, along with the gratin, to make Sunday a little less frantic. This also meant that I could scrape off some fat that was sitting on top of the duck. Fat is to duck as hormones are to teenagers: it oozes out of them.

Using duck legs is a good way to serve duck to more than a few people if you have an eye on the purse-strings: it's much cheaper to buy all legs than two whole ducks, and there's also no need to get the carving knife out. I served this dish with two root vegetable side dishes and some spinach for a flash of green. I don't offer a recipe for the spinach: just wash it, drain it in a colander and throw it in a hot pan, lid on. It'll only take a minute or two to wilt, then you just need to drain it of any excess water and chop it up a bit. Add a little seasoning, butter and maybe some nutmeg, if you wish.

6 duck legs

18 shallots, peeled and left whole

2 garlic cloves, peeled and crushed

1 tablespoon plain flour

450ml port

200ml chicken stock (fresh, or made from a good-quality liquid bouillon)

finely grated zest and juice of 1 orange

10 juniper berries, crushed

6 sprigs of thyme

200g cranberries, fresh or frozen

3 tablespoons ready-made redcurrant jelly

2 tablespoons granulated sugar

salt and pepper

Heat up a big frying pan without any oil and brown the duck legs (they may need to go in the pan in batches). Remove the duck legs to a large roasting tin, then add the shallots and garlic to the pan, stirring now and then in the fat emitted by the duck – you are aiming for a nice caramel colour. (Incidentally, if the thought of peeling all those shallots sends you reaching for the tissues, pop them in a pan of boiling water for a couple of minutes before you do so: it takes the sting out of them and the skins come off much more easily.)

Once the shallots and garlic have had their frying time, add them to the duck legs. Check the oil level in the pan; some fat will have come out of the duck, so pour off all but 1 tablespoon but don't discard what's been poured off. Pour it into a small bowl and pop it in the fridge – it's a roast potato's best friend. Add the flour to the remaining tablespoon of fat and stir for a couple of minutes before adding the port and the stock. Finally, add the rest of the ingredients and pour them over the duck in the roasting tin.

You can either cook the dish then and there at 200°C/Gas Mark 6 for an hour, or else refrigerate it and bring it to room temperature before cooking it the next day. The finished dish, with its sprigs of green thyme and flaming cranberry jewels, is a pageant to all the holly and berries that are still to come.

Celeriac and Potato Gratin

The duck is fruity; this is creamy. Perfect partners.

500g floury maincrop potatoes, such as King Edwards or Maris Piper
400g celeriac
50g butter
4 garlic cloves, peeled and crushed
salt and pepper
287ml double cream
just over 300ml full-fat milk (you need enough to make the cream up to 600ml)

Peel the potatoes and the celeriac and put them in cold water until you are ready to slice them. Ideally, you should use a mandolin for this (a gadget you will always find being wielded with great showmanship and aplomb in department stores and at food shows), but if you use one, do take care with it. The Vicar is 'Mandolin Man' in my house, but once he cockily didn't bother to use the safety guard. As well as carrots, the top of his finger ended up in the soup. And, yes, I did serve it. Anyway, slice the vegetables up into thin discs and keep them separate, putting them back into some fresh cold water to stop them turning brown.

Lightly butter a shallow ovenproof dish that measures approximately 26cm x 22cm and layer the potato and celeriac in alternate layers, sprinkling some garlic and salt and pepper over each layer. Finally, pour the cream into a measuring jug and make it up to 600ml with the milk. Pour the milk and cream over the vegetables, dot with the remaining butter, and bake for $2^{1}/_{4}$ hours at 150°C/Gas Mark 2.

Celeriac and Potato Mash

I chose to make a celeriac and potato gratin, as I have two ovens, but if you only have one, a celeriac and potato mash would do just as well.

1kg floury maincrop potatoes, such as King Edwards or Maris Piper
500g celeriac
70g butter

3 tablespoons double cream
6 tablespoons full-fat milk
salt and pepper

Peel the potatoes and the celeriac and cut them evenly into medium-sized chunks. Pop them into separate pans of boiling salted water and cook until soft. The celeriac should take around 15 minutes, the potatoes, 20–25 minutes. Meanwhile, heat up the butter, cream and milk in another pan.

When the vegetables are ready, drain them in a colander, add to the hot dairy-fest in the other pan and mash together, adding salt and pepper to taste. The mash can be whisked with an electric whisk to make it light and fluffy, if you wish.

serves 6

Turnips and Leeks with Honey, Coriander and Soy

2 tablespoons olive oil

30g butter

12 large turnips, cut into 2cm cubes

2 garlic cloves, peeled and crushed

2 teaspoons coriander seeds, crushed

3 leeks, cleaned and chopped into 2cm lengths

2 tablespoons light soy sauce

1 tablespoon runny honey

salt and pepper

Heat the oil and butter in a large pan and toss in the turnips, stirring so that they are evenly coated in the hot fat. Cook the turnips for 15 minutes, stirring occasionally, then add the garlic and coriander seeds. When the turnips are virtually soft, add the leeks and put a lid on the pan.

Cook for around 8 minutes more – you want the leeks to be soft, not crispy. Finally, add the soy sauce and honey and stir to coat the vegetables. Season, but don't go wild with the salt as the soy sauce is quite salty anyway.

Winter Fruit Pie

Easy peasy, this. Always a lover of the shortcut, I used bought puff pastry and it tasted just fine, indeed, far better than any I could have attempted, I'm sure. Feel free to be flexible with the fruit; just use whatever is around.

5 apples, peeled, quartered and cored

2 large pears, peeled, quartered and cored

5 plums, halved and the stones removed

4 tablespoons brown sugar

1 tablespoon granulated sugar

60g butter

150g golden syrup

375g bought puff pastry, chilled (mine was ready-rolled)

1 egg, beaten

custard or cream (single or double), to serve

Take the apples and slice each quarter into 3 and cut the pears into similar-sized chunks. Put the apples and pears in a pan with 2 tablespoons of water and cook for 10 minutes or until soft. Meanwhile, cut each of the plum halves into 4 and put them in a shallow, 2-litre baking dish with a rim. Add the apples and pears when they are done, including any remaining water.

Put both types of sugar, the butter and golden syrup in a pan and heat it until bubbling. Pour this foaming lava over the fruit and then brush the rim of the dish with water/beaten egg. If you haven't bought ready-rolled pastry, roll it out on a lightly floured surface. Lay the pastry over the top of the dish, press it onto the rim well and trim away any excess pastry, if necessary. Pinch round the edges of the pie to give it an attractive finish, prick the pastry with a fork and brush with more of the egg. The pie will take around 45 minutes to cook in an oven set at 200°C/Gas Mark 6. Serve with custard or cream.

serves 6

An alternative Christmas lunch

The Vicar says there is only one reason why we eat turkey only once a year. I don't think I need to elaborate … On the Christmases that we have stayed at home, we have steered clear of turkey and opted for an alternative. One year, four days after my son's arrival into the world, it was sea bass and crab-mashed potato. Two years later, with my daughter, Greta's, splendidly timed delivery on Christmas Eve, it was duck. If we have another Christmas at home, I think I'd plump for partridge, and I'd serve it with a pear and onion confit to conjure up the 12 days of Christmas and partridges in pear trees. After I'd come up with this oh-so-original and witty idea, I spotted Nigel Slater had hit on the very same combination in that weekend's *Observer*. The man's a genius.

PARTRIDGE WITH PEAR AND ONION CONFIT

PANCETTA COLCANNON

THE TRIMMINGS

TANGERINE SURPRISE PUDDING

serves 4

Partridge with Pear and Onion Confit

Partridges are compact little birds with a powerful, gamey smell. To put it less politely, they honk. However, get past this and they make a lovely feast dish.

4 organic partridges
8 slices of rindless, smoked streaky
    bacon
125ml red wine
125ml vegetable stock (I use the
    water reserved from cooking the
    vegetables)
1 teaspoon ready-made cranberry
    sauce
salt and pepper

For the pear and onion confit:
20g butter
1 onion, peeled and finely chopped
40g granulated sugar
2 pears, peeled, quartered, cored
    and cut into 1cm cubes
30ml water
40ml white wine vinegar
salt and pepper

First, crack on with the pear and onion confit, as you need to serve it at room temperature. Melt the butter in a pan and add the onion and sugar. Cook at a fairly low heat for 5 minutes or until the onion is soft, but not brown. Now add the pears and stir to coat with the buttery juices. Pour in the water and vinegar and let it all bubble away for 15–20 minutes or until the liquid has reduced and looks glossy and syrupy. Season and pour into a bowl ready for serving.

Now for the partridges. Put the partridges in a small roasting tin and cover each one with 2 slices of bacon. Cook in an oven preheated to 200°C/Gas Mark 6 for about 45 minutes. They may still have a pink tinge to them after this amount of time, so if you prefer a well-done bird, cook them for a few minutes more.

When the partridges are ready, remove them to a warmed serving plate, cover with foil and set aside somewhere warm. Then place the roasting tin over a medium heat on the hob and scrape up any juicy bits from the bottom of the tin. Add the wine and let it boil away furiously until reduced by about half, then add the stock, cranberry sauce and seasoning and simmer for a few minutes until reduced to a well-flavoured gravy. Pour into a gravy boat and serve.

Pancetta Colcannon

This is a perfect way to embrace tradition, and yet improve on it. Whilst Christmas lunch screams Brussels sprouts, I don't know many people who rave about them. Here they are grated into mash festooned with smoked bacon lardons, and the whole thing slips down a treat. I first served it to an Irish friend and her husband, and it turned out that they had lived for some years in the place in southern Ireland where the Vicar and I had spent a rather windswept honeymoon. So as we ate our colcannon, we reminisced fondly about the emerald land of leprechauns, Guinness and abundant potatoes.

The quantity below would serve six, but leftovers make fabulous bubble and squeak patties. (See page 302 for a cabbage version and a rather delicious sauce.)

120g butter
250g Brussels sprouts, trimmed and coarsely grated (use a food processor, if you have one)
1kg floury maincrop potatoes, such as King Edwards or Maris Piper

200g cubed pancetta or smoked bacon lardons
100ml double cream
salt and pepper

Melt 50g of the butter in a frying pan and fry the sprouts for around 7 minutes until soft, then set aside.

Meanwhile, peel the potatoes and cut them into medium-sized chunks. Pop them into a pan of boiling salted water and cook for 20–25 minutes or until soft. While they are busy cooking, heat up another frying pan and fry the pancetta or bacon until some bits look crispy. (You don't need any oil here, as the meat will ooze out on its own and it will fry itself in it.)

Heat up the cream and the rest of the butter in a separate pan, and when the potatoes are ready, drain them well, add them to butter and cream mixture and mash it all together. Stir in the grated sprouts and pancetta and season well. Heat through, if necessary, before eating.

The Trimmings

Roast parsnips: Goodness, it's up to you, but I can't have Christmas without roast parsnips. Parboil them for 5 minutes and, even though they aren't potatoes, I still distress them, bumping them merrily up and down in my metal colander with a pan lid on top. Meanwhile, heat up 1 tablespoon of oil on the hob until it's snapping at you and toss the parsnips in it. Cook at 210°C/Gas Mark 7 or until soft in the middle and toffee-crunchy on the outside.

Chipolatas: *Go to your butcher*, or buy good ones. And remember, people scoff more of these than you think is possible. Think at least 4 per person – leftovers will not be a problem, I promise. Cook them in the bottom of the oven, anointed with drizzles of oil. If they are not brown when you are ready to serve, just pop them under the grill. If you want to add 1 tablespoon of honey and the same of wholegrain mustard to them before they exit the oven, feel free.

Green vegetables: Broccoli, cabbage – whatever. Just don't drink too much Champagne/sherry and overcook them.

Tangerine Surprise Pudding

One of my first experiments in the kitchen was a lemon surprise pudding. At age sixteen it wasn't a great success and didn't hint of any kitchen prowess in the making. Thankfully, I've honed my skills since then and this is my version for Christmas time. It's zesty and surprisingly light. Any leftovers can be eaten with a coffee the next day. Indeed, I would be quite happy with it for breakfast.

100g butter, softened
200g caster sugar
finely grated zest of 4 tangerines
4 medium eggs, separated
75g plain flour, sifted
100ml tangerine juice
juice of 1 small lemon (about 3 tablespoons)
500ml full-fat milk
custard, or single cream, to serve (optional)

Lightly butter a 2-litre shallow ovenproof dish and preheat the oven to 180°C/Gas Mark 4.

In a large mixing bowl, whisk together the butter and sugar and tangerine zest until it lightens in colour. It won't go all lovely and fluffy, so don't carry on whisking *ad infinitum*. Separate the eggs, putting the whites into a large, clean bowl and the yolks into a cup. Lightly beat the egg yolks with a fork and gradually whisk them into the creamed butter mixture, bit by bit. Now sift over the flour and beat it in a spoonful at a time, alternating with slurps of the juices and milk.

Using a clean, dry, electric whisk, whisk the egg whites until they rise in soft peaks. Fold into the pudding, ignoring the rather grainy consistency (don't worry, you haven't done it wrong).

Put the dish into a *bain-marie* (a roasting tin or another dish), and pour in hot, not boiling water to come halfway up the sides of the dish. Cook in the oven for 40–45 minutes or until the top looks golden brown and set. Serve with cream or custard.

I know that the fact I like to invite people to a dinner party sounds as though I'm stuck in the 80s (or 70s, even), but sometimes I want to give family or friends a bit of a treat, to indulge them a little. Laying on dinner is the main way in which I do that: it's the chance to serve nice drinks and to be able to sit around a table that has been ever so slightly primped and polished – all of which gives the evening more of a sense of occasion than your usual homely, workaday supper. I'm not necessarily suggesting that you bring out the posh china or freshly laundered napkins, nor am I demanding that people dress up, but a delicious, carefully thought-out dinner that's been designed to please and pamper is a wonderful thing. It is, for everyone, the culinary equivalent of being given a beautiful present, a relaxing massage, or even a full-blown visit to a spa. And if you want to throw in some nice music and a couple of candles to add to the therapeutic ambience, that's really up to you.

Dinner For Friends

Fish

When I was a vegetarian, I could never have given up eating fish: I love it too much. For me, wandering around a vast fish market awash with gleaming scales, glittering eyes and pile upon pile of sparkling shellfish is one of life's magical moments – I almost have to stop myself from bursting into a bad rendition of 'All Things Bright and Beautiful'. I also relish the buying of fresh fish: the choosing and pointing; the flash of the sharp knives; the constant splash of fresh, icy water. I am also, oddball that I am, curiously fond of the white paper my fish gets wrapped in.

And then there's the cooking. I have to admit that I rather enjoy the faint tension that cooking fish brings, the anxiety that having spent a certain amount of money on your dinner, you are now about to ruin it. Fish, after all, demands a light hand and a sharp eye on the clock. As long as one remembers this, it's a joy to prepare and is the ideal fast food. None of the recipes in this section takes long to make, so you could easily knock them up for a midweek splurge (they aren't intended to be prepared ahead of time). For some reason, I always crave fish more in the warmer months, so most of these menus have a fairly summery feel. That's not to say that fish is banned in the winter in my house, it's just that when it's cold outside I want to eat something a little less elegant than a rather refined sea bass or a delicate piece of sole. Come a touch of chill and I need my fish to be more rustic and coated in some sort of gloopy comfort, such as sauces, cheese and good-old mashed potato.

A dinner to delight the senses

A summer's evening and it's dinner on the terrace for four. It's me, the Vicar, and another couple. I wanted to serve a main course that was fresh, light and full of zing. After that, I was after a contrasting pudding: something luxurious and wickedly creamy. Come to think of it, if you halved everything, this meal would make fabulous seduction food. Actually, don't halve the pudding: scoff the lot.

GUACAMOLE-ENCRUSTED TUNA

ROASTED RED ONION AND TOMATOES

GRIDDLED COURGETTES IN GARLIC AND PARSLEY DRESSING

WHITE CHOCOLATE AND RASPBERRY CRÈME BRÛLÉE

Guacamole-encrusted Tuna

I love tuna, but only if it's cooked to perfection. For me, that means rare, but hot all the way through. It's quite a tricky culinary feat to pull off; tuna steaks coming in various shapes and sizes, and all. Too little time on the griddle and the fish ends up cold in the middle; too much, and you might as well feed it to the cat.

I remember one particularly bad tuna event some years back at some friends' house. The male half of the couple proudly announced that he was cooking tuna niçoise, and we all spent a fair few minutes making bonding murmurs about the necessity for it to be cooked just-so. The Vicar and I joined the chef in the kitchen as he cheerfully set about his task. Salad made; dressing prepared; on went the tuna. Two minutes passed; five minutes passed; ten minutes passed. By now the Vicar and I could barely still hold a conversation, transfixed, we stared in sad horror as the still-happy chef carried out tuna cremation. After fifteen minutes, Cardboard Niçoise was finally on the table. A memorable meal.

Here is a tuna dish that I hope will stick in your minds for all the right reasons: it's colourful, light, yet full of flavour and beautiful to behold. I used to hate guacamole (and if it is shop-bought I still do; it looks like a terrifyingly toxic substance exuded by aliens from *Doctor Who*); homemade, however, is a different matter. There's texture, and the combination of the soft mildness of the avocado, the heat of the chilli, the zinginess of the lime and the fragrance of the coriander is addictive. The tuna doesn't take very long to cook, so do prepare any other dishes first.

4 spring onions or ½ small red onion, peeled and finely chopped
juice of 4 limes
2 tablespoons coriander, chopped
4–5 teaspoons red chilli (fresh, or 'Lazy Chilli' from a jar), de-seeded and finely chopped

2 large or 4 small ripe avocados, peeled and stoned
salt and pepper
2 small packets plain tortilla chips
4 spankingly fresh tuna steaks (each weighing about 175–200g)

To make the guacamole, all you need to do is pile the spring onions, lime juice, coriander, chilli, avocados and seasoning into a bowl and mash them together. Don't go wild, though, as you want a bit of lumpiness going on to avoid any reminders of alien pus (sorry, now I've probably put you off your food). These quantities make too much guacamole for the tuna recipe, so feel free to graze a bit as you cook.

Heat up the griddle or frying pan over a high heat until it's smoking hot. Meanwhile, bash the bags of tortilla chips with a rolling pin, which, if you have a childish bone in your body, is a job you'll enjoy. It'll make you want to get another bag and do that fantastically irritating banging thing that makes the crisp bag burst open and drives sensible adults totally mad. Anyway, toast

the crumbs lightly in another, dry, frying pan and watch them like a hawk –
you want them to be lightly golden, not burnt.

Meanwhile, griddle the tuna steaks on each side. For tuna steaks about $1\frac{1}{2}$cm
thick, I would go for $1\frac{1}{2}$ minutes on each side, maybe slightly less. If they're
thicker, they will obviously need a bit longer. Remove from the pan and
spread each steak with a thick carpet of guacamole, then sprinkle over the
tortilla crumbs to make a crust. Serve with the roasted red onions and
tomatoes and the dressed courgettes and eat, maybe with a glass of chilled
rosé wine.

Roasted Red Onion and Tomatoes

6 large, vine-ripened tomatoes,
  halved
2 red onions, peeled and quartered
4 garlic cloves, peeled and crushed

4 tablespoons basil oil
salt and pepper
1 tablespoon balsamic vinegar

Arrange the tomatoes and onions in a roasting tin, sprinkle over the garlic and basil oil and season generously with salt and pepper. Pop the dish in an oven preheated to 200°C/Gas Mark 6. The vegetables need to cook for 25–30 minutes or until they are nicely browned and tender, at which point you can swirl in 1 tablespoon of the balsamic vinegar. Turn the oven down low, to about 120°C/Gas Mark ½, and put the dish back in whilst you finish off preparing the rest of the feast.

serves 4

Griddled Courgettes in Garlic and Parsley Dressing

2 courgettes
olive oil, for brushing
6 tablespoons lemon oil
2 tablespoons lemon juice

2 garlic cloves, peeled and crushed
salt and pepper
2 tablespoons flatleaf parsley,
  chopped

Halve the courgettes widthways, then slice each half lengthways into thin slices. Brush them with some olive oil and either sear them in a frying pan or griddle them on a ridged grill pan, if you have one, so that you get those nice, brown ridge marks that make you feel ever so slightly chef-like.

Once the courgettes are cooked, put them on a plate and pop it in the warm oven to keep the tomatoes company. Combine the lemon oil and lemon juice in a small bowl, add the garlic and seasoning and stir together thoroughly. When you are ready to serve, slather it over the courgettes and sprinkle over the parsley.

White Chocolate and Raspberry Crème Brûlée

This luxurious pudding provides a fantastic contrast to the fresh-tasting main course. It needs to be made in advance (bar the caramelising bit), which means that once the tuna is dealt with, you can relax and lap up the fabulous pleasures of good food and friends.

225g fresh raspberries
200g good-quality white chocolate
400ml double cream

5 egg yolks
1 tablespoon caster sugar
about 100g demerara sugar

Divide the raspberries among the bases of four ramekins or small shallow dishes of about 9cm in diameter. You may not need all of the fruit, depending on the size of your dishes, but keep any that's left over to serve on the side. Pop all four dishes into the freezer.

Break the white chocolate into a bowl placed over a pan of just simmering water and leave to cook until glossily molten and smooth. Take care not to let the bowl touch the water or let it get too hot, or the chocolate will go grainy. Heat the double cream in a small pan until hand-hot. Whisk the yolks and caster sugar in a bowl for a couple of minutes, then carefully pour the hot cream on to the yolks and whisk together. Pour the mixture through a sieve back into a clean pan and stir over a low heat for about 5 minutes or until the custard is very thick. Remove from the heat, add the melted chocolate and mix together until smooth. Leave to cool for about 10 minutes and then pour the mixture into the ramekins. Cover and chill in the fridge overnight or until set.

serves 4

Once set, sprinkle the tops of the brûlées with the demerara sugar and spray with a little water, which helps the sugar to caramelise. (You can buy water sprays at garden centres, or places like Ikea.) Blast the tops of the puddings with a blowtorch or place the ramekins under a hot grill until the sugar is a beautiful golden brown. Chill in the fridge for 30 minutes before serving.

A goodbye dinner of effortless elegance

Summer has nearly left London, and so too have some friends of ours, who are moving. To say a goodbye to both I cooked a delicately delicious, late-summer dinner that had one of my guests vigorously and unashamedly scraping his plate clean.

WARM SMOKED TROUT FILLETS IN A HORSERADISH AND CHIVE CREAM SAUCE

GARLICKY POTATOES IN ROSEMARY AND PANCETTA

GREEN AND RED SALAD

LAVENDER SHORTBREAD WITH BLACKBERRIES IN MUSCAT AND LEMON CREAM

Warm Smoked Trout Fillets in a Horseradish and Chive Cream Sauce

8 fillets of hot-smoked trout
15g butter
1 shallot, peeled and finely chopped
150ml white wine
200ml double cream

2 teaspoons horseradish cream
juice of $\frac{1}{2}$ lemon
1 tablespoon chives, chopped
salt and pepper

The trout needs little preparation: it only needs to be heated through just before serving. I know many people despise the microwave, but it's a very convenient tool for something like this. Trout fillets are quite delicate little creatures, so rather than heat them in an oven in a baking tray (they'd take around 10–12 minutes at 160°C/Gas Mark 3) and then have to oh-so-carefully transfer them to warm plates, I found it easier to put the cold fillets on their plates and zap them in the microwave for 90 seconds per plate. Hot fillets and hot plates in one easy step! I did this as the sauce was reaching its final stages and put the prepared plates of fish in the oven to keep their heat once they'd had their time in the microwave.

To make the sauce, melt the butter in a medium-sized pan and cook the shallot until soft but not brown. Pour in the wine and let it reduce for 6–7 minutes until fairly syrupy. Add the cream, and again let it reduce a bit before adding the rest of the ingredients. Season well and pour over the fish. Eat with the green and red salad and garlicky potatoes and feel free to lick your plates.

Garlicky Potatoes in Rosemary and Pancetta

750g floury maincrop potatoes, such as King Edwards or Maris Piper

3 tablespoons olive oil

3 garlic cloves, peeled and crushed

3 sprigs of rosemary, leaves pulled off the stalks

60g cubed pancetta or smoked bacon lardons

salt and pepper

Prepare the potatoes first. Wash them, dry them in some kitchen towel, then cut them into 2cm chunks. Pop them in a roasting tin with the oil, garlic and rosemary.

Preheat the oven to 200°C/Gas Mark 6. Meanwhile, fry the pancetta lightly (no oil needed). Toss this in with the potatoes, season with salt and pepper and put in the oven. They should take about 45 minutes. When done, the potatoes should be pleasingly crispy on the outside and fluffy in the middle, which, incidentally, is just how I like my chips.

Green and Red Salad

1 large red onion, peeled
3 tablespoons extra virgin olive oil
1 tablespoon red wine vinegar
1 garlic clove, peeled and crushed
1 teaspoon French mustard
salt and pepper
pinch of granulated sugar
125g baby asparagus spears or
   French beans, trimmed

a large handful of sugar snaps
7 sweet baby plum tomatoes, halved
1 tablespoon flatleaf parsley,
   chopped
1 tablespoon basil leaves, torn into
   small pieces

For the salad, cut the onion in half lengthways through the root, then across into 5mm thick slices and separate them into rings. Toss the red onion rings in a roasting tin with 1 tablespoon of the olive oil and put in the oven on the shelf below the potatoes (still set to 200°C/Gas Mark 6). They will only need about 10 minutes in there to sweeten and soften up. When the onion rings are ready, put the rest of the olive oil and the vinegar, garlic, mustard, seasoning and sugar into a salad bowl and whisk everything together to combine. Add the roasted onions, oil and all.

Cook the asparagus spears for 3 minutes in salted boiling water (French beans will take slightly longer – 4 minutes or so or until they still have bite, but aren't raw), adding the sugar snaps for the last minute or so of the cooking time. Drain the vegetables and add them, still warm, to the salad bowl. Leave the salad on the side whilst you get on with the fishy bit. Just before serving, add the tomatoes and herbs to the bowl and toss everything together.

Lavender Shortbread with Blackberries in Muscat and Lemon Cream

Apart from the shortbread, this dessert is a bit of a cheat. I included the lavender in the biscuits to pick up on the purple colour of the blackberries and to add a note of mysterious scentiness. To adorn the top of the biscuits, I naughtily plucked a sprig of fresh lavender from someone's front garden down the road. Unfortunately, my son saw me and copied my evil actions a few doors down, gleefully grabbing a bundle of leaves from a rather attractive plant. There's nothing like leading by example. The poor child was spotted mid-theft by the Vicar and scolded, to my very great shame.

The blackberries need only be warmed through in the sweet, honeyed wine and the lemon cream is just good lemon curd mixed with Greek yogurt. But there's no need to divulge these secrets if you don't want to; just sit back and watch people enjoy the pleasing combination of some tender blackberries, a creamy yet zesty mousse, and a nice crisp biscuit. Or maybe two.

For the lavender shortbread:
olive oil, for greasing
160g plain flour
15g semolina
100g butter
1 teaspoon dried lavender (or finely
    chopped fresh)
50g caster sugar
finely grated zest of 1 lemon
2 teaspoons lemon juice

For the blackberries in Muscat:
450g blackberries
100ml sweet dessert wine, such as
    Muscat de Beaumes de Venise or
    the far cheaper Moscatel de
    Valencia
1 tablespoon caster sugar

For the lemon cream:
400g Greek natural yogurt
4 tablespoons good-quality lemon
    curd

Preheat the oven to 160°C/Gas Mark 3. For the lavender shortbread, wipe a little oil over two baking trays and then sift the flour into a large bowl, followed by the semolina. Cut the butter into chunks and stir in. You could use a food processor to combine all this together, but if you can't be bothered to get it out, rub in the butter with your fingertips, allowing the mixture to fall through your fingers. Continue until it looks like fine breadcrumbs and then stir in the lavender, sugar and lemon zest and juice. Using your hands, form the mixture into a ball and then place it on a lightly floured surface. Roll out the dough with a floured rolling pin until it is about 5mm thick, and then cut out lots of little shapes using mini-sized cutters. (I used a star shape and a heart shape.)

Using a spatula or a palette knife, lift the biscuits onto the baking trays, re-kneading and rolling out any scraps until all the dough has been used. Bake for 12–15 minutes until crisp and lightly golden, then place on a wire rack to cool.

For the blackberries, put the fruit, wine and sugar into a pan and stir over a low heat until the sugar has disappeared and the blackberries are hot but not collapsing.

For the lemon cream, simply stir the Greek yogurt and lemon curd together. Serve with the blackberries and lavender shortbreads or eat on its own as a lemon mousse.

Million-dollar dinner

Whilst this dinner doesn't cost a king's ransom to produce, it's luxurious, delicious and makes you feel that you are richer than you really are. If, in reality, you aren't hugely wealthy, can I beg you to remind yourself of the fact as soon as you can after finishing eating? I'd hate to be the one to blame if, full of this sumptuous food, you rush out and buy a Porsche.

The dessert is my twist on that old-fashioned classic, Peach Melba. I remember eating cheap café versions of it as a child: tinned peaches and sickly sauce, served with bad-quality ice cream. I served my version on one big white plate and gave everyone a spoon – which was a bad idea as a physical fight nearly ensued. Unfortunately, one greedy person (okay, actually it was my spouse) felt he had the right to try and hoover up everything from left, right and centre. 'Get off!' came the outraged cry from the woman to his left, 'That's *my* sauce!'

Please note that the peaches need to be served at room temperature, so you should bake them a little in advance to allow them time to cool down. You could also prepare the raspberry purée ahead of time.

PLAICE IN SOURED CREAM AND CHIVES

BABY JERSEY ROYAL POTATOES IN CAVIAR

BAKED PEACHES IN SPIKED RASPBERRY PURÉE

Plaice in Soured Cream and Chives and Baby Jersey Royal Potatoes in Caviar

4 large, or 8 small, spankingly fresh
    fillets of plaice
salt and pepper
6 tablespoons crème fraîche
3 tablespoons chives, chopped (I use
    kitchen scissors, it's loads easier)
juice of 1½ lemons
3 garlic cloves, peeled and crushed

For the potatoes:
500g baby Jersey Royal potatoes
big slice of butter, about 25g
4 teaspoons lumpfish caviar or
    salmon keta
black pepper
4 big handfuls of baby spinach
    leaves

Take your lovely shiny pieces of plaice, lay them out in a baking dish and season liberally. Then mix the crème fraîche with the chives, lemon juice and garlic and a really generous grinding of salt and pepper, and spread this mixture over the fish. The potatoes and the fish will both take 20–25 minutes to cook, so put the potatoes in a pan of salted boiling water and pop the fish in an oven preheated to 200°C/Gas Mark 6. You could now tidy up a bit or else defiantly turn your back on any kitchen mess and go and have a nice chilled glass of wine with your guests, which is obviously the polite option.

When the cooking time is up (keep your eye on the clock), drain those beautiful potatoes and anoint them with a generous amount of butter, the caviar or salmon keta and some black pepper (no salt, though, as the caviar is quite salty enough). The plaice is cooked when it has lost any hint of translucency, but you want it to remain moist and tender. Keep an eye on it during the cooking time if you are at all worried.

Serve each person with a plaice fillet and some sauce, some potatoes and a handful of baby spinach. I don't think you should dress the leaves – they are there for colour and to mop up any stray bits of sauce or caviar butter.

serves 4

Baked Peaches in Spiked Raspberry Purée

4 ripe peaches, halved and the
    stones removed
8 teaspoons demerara sugar
250g fresh raspberries
2 tablespoons icing sugar

a good splash of vodka, about
    2 tablespoons
some good-quality vanilla ice
    cream, to serve

Preheat the oven to 200°C/Gas Mark 6. Place the peaches flesh-side up in a shallow baking dish and sprinkle each half with 1 teaspoon of the demerara sugar. Now splash each half with about 2 teaspoons of cold water and cook the peaches in the oven for around 25 minutes. The peaches are ready when they are tender when pierced with a sharp knife. Allow to cool.

For the purée, combine the raspberries with the icing sugar and put the whole lot in a blender and whizz. Now push the purée through a sieve into a small pan, add the vodka and warm gently over a low heat. Swirl it over the peaches and serve with the vanilla ice cream. It'll look beautiful and taste so, too.

A treat for food-loving friends

A trip to the fishmonger's and I am very many pounds lighter – financially, that is. But that's okay, this dinner was always meant to be a treat; a chance to spoil tired friends who don't earn very much but really appreciate lovely food. It turned out to be a very happy, laid-back evening. Indeed, one old friend relaxed so much that, by the time pudding was finished, he was fast asleep, head on the table, snoring loudly. He rang up the next day to say thank you and apologise 'for the lack of service towards the end'.

Like the main course, the pudding is a bit special, too. For a start, gooseberries are only really around for a few brief weeks in the summer, so eating them always feels like a celebration in its own right. You could also make this pudding with other fruit, such as blackberries, which you wouldn't need to cook in the pan or add sugar to. But the combination of slightly tart gooseberries and elderflower-scented creamy custard is something that is really rather hard to beat.

PAN-ROASTED HALIBUT ON CLAM STEW

GOOSEBERRY AND ELDERFLOWER CUSTARD

Pan-roasted Halibut on Clam Stew

I often buy mussels, but hardly ever clams. However, having eaten some on holiday in Spain, I decided to give them a go. I tracked down the *palourdes* (also known as carpetshell clams) at my local fishmonger, which are bigger than some other varieties. You may want to give your fishmonger a ring to check if he has them in or if he can order some for you. If you can't get clams, use mussels instead.

1kg fresh clams (*palourdes*)
4 tablespoons olive oil
1 onion, peeled and finely chopped
1 heaped teaspoon red chilli (fresh, or use 'Lazy Chilli' from a jar), de-seeded and finely chopped
3 garlic cloves, peeled and chopped
250ml white wine

900ml passata
6 fillets of halibut or any other meaty white fish, each weighing about 200g
2 tablespoons parsley, chopped
1 tablespoon basil leaves, torn up
juice of ½ lemon
salt and pepper

When you've got your bag of shellfish home, empty it into a big bowl of cold water and discard any shells that are open. (It's probably unnecessary to remind you not to eat any that are tight shut once you've cooked them. However, I once cooked some mussels and absent-mindedly prised one open at the dinner table and ate it. Let's say I didn't sleep much that night.) In a big, deep, flameproof pan (I used my trusty witch's cauldron), heat 2 tablespoons of the oil and then add the onion, chilli and garlic. Fry gently for about 5 minutes until the onion has softened, but not browned. Throw in the clams, pour over the wine and bring to the boil. When you can see it bubbling away, add the passata and cook for about five minutes or until the clams are open.

Meanwhile, pour the rest of the olive oil into a frying pan and place on a high heat. Once the oil is really hot, lower in the fish, skin-side down and cook for about 4 minutes. (I chose halibut as it is a meaty fish which, unlike cod, doesn't fall apart when it's cooked. It is a bit of a treat, though, being devilishly expensive.) Have a little peek at the skin now and again, as you are aiming for brown and crispy. Gently turn the fish over and cook for around 30 seconds more, then turn off the heat.

It's handy to get one of your guests involved at some point in the end stages of cooking, preferably someone who doesn't mind getting a bit mucky (don't go for anyone wearing white or dry clean only!). The friend needs to de-shell as many clams from the big pan as he/she can manage, removing the shells and discarding them. Not all of them need this treatment, as some unshelled clams in the stew look pretty, it's just that if they are all in the shells the dish is a bit of a faff to eat, and some people can't abide food that needs a lot of fiddling with before they can actually get it in their mouths.

Before serving the stew, add the herbs and lemon juice and test for seasoning, adding pepper but being restrained with the salt as the clams have their own sea-salty taste. Serve the stew in big flat bowls, with the fish placed on top, skin-side up. All you need to accompany it is some good bread.

Gooseberry and Elderflower Custard

Oh, it took me endless trouble to get this recipe right. I wanted the custard to be set, but not overly firm. The first one I attempted was too runny and the second had lost all its unctuous wobble. I kept trying because the taste of the thing was so beautiful that I really wanted to get it right. And here you have it. Prepare it before your guests arrive, as it is best served at room temperature and making it will require all your attention.

350g gooseberries (or, out of season, use a 350g jar of bottled gooseberries and then only 3 tablespoons of cordial)

5 tablespoons elderflower cordial
6 large egg yolks
50g caster sugar
500ml double cream

You will need one shallow gratin dish, about 1.2 litres in capacity.

Pull the little fluffy stalks off the gooseberries and discard, then wash the fruit in a colander or sieve. Pop them in a pan and add 2 tablespoons of the elderflower cordial. Put the gooseberries on a medium heat and cook until they start to pop and the juices are syrupy; this should only take a few minutes. Drain them of any liquid and discard it, tip the gooseberries into the gratin dish and set aside so you can crack on with the custard. (If you are using gooseberries from a jar, there is no need to cook them: just drain them of their juice and put them straight into the gratin dish.)

Briefly whisk the egg yolks in a large bowl with the sugar, then heat the double cream and the rest of the elderflower cordial in a small pan until boiling. Pour the scented cream onto the egg yolks and sugar, stirring constantly, then pour the whole lot back into the pan. Cook on a gentle heat, stirring constantly, for about 5 minutes or until the mixture is thick enough to coat the back of a wooden spoon. Now strain the custard through a sieve into a large bowl, which ensures a really smooth custard, and pour it over the gooseberries.

Put the dish in a *bain-marie* (that's a baking dish filled with enough hot – but not boiling – water to come up to halfway up the sides of the gratin dish) and bake in a preheated oven at 150°C/Gas Mark 2 until lightly set. It should take about 25–30 minutes, but check it after 25 minutes and turn the oven down to 140°C/Gas Mark 1 if the top is beginning to colour. When cooked it should still have a wobble in the centre; it will firm up as it cools. Remove and leave on the side until you are ready to eat.

A rather posh pasta night

Scallops are one of my favourite things and they combine beautifully with bacon. They don't come cheap, though, so feel free to buy fewer than I specify if you are trying to save cash. Or, to save even more money, just halve everything and cook it for yourself and someone you love very much (and if you're feeling very greedy, this other person could even be you).

TAGLIOLINI WITH SALMON, SCALLOPS AND PANCETTA

BAKED APRICOTS WITH AMARETTI BISCUITS

Tagliolini with Salmon, Scallops and Pancetta

1 tablespoon olive oil
170g pancetta, cut into small cubes
30g butter
2 salmon fillets, each weighing
    around 180–200g, cut into 2cm
    chunks
400g scallops, cleaned and removed
    from their shells

125ml white wine
2 tablespoons parsley, chopped
juice of ½ lemon
salt and pepper
a small knob of butter (optional)
300g fresh tagliolini (or you could
    use linguine, spaghetti, or even
    tagliatelle)

Bring a large pan of salted water to the boil. Heat the oil in a large frying pan over a medium-high heat and add the pancetta. Cook for a couple of minutes and then add the butter. Once it's frothing, add the salmon and cook for about 1½ minutes, then turn the chunks over and add the scallops. Cook them for 1½ minutes, turn over and cook for another minute. Pour in the wine, let it come to the boil and bubble away and then throw in the parsley, lemon juice and the seasoning. Add the butter if you want to add a bit of gloss to the sauce.

Meanwhile, cook your pasta in the pan of boiling water: follow the cooking instructions on the packet, but if it's fresh it should only take a few minutes. Drain the pasta well and toss with the sauce. Serve in big, flat, warmed, individual bowls.

serves 4

Baked Apricots with Amaretti Biscuits

This dessert makes a good contrast to the creamy main course, is very easy to prepare, and brings the best out of apricots – which when raw are, in this country at least, a tough and tasteless disappointment. These babies are the opposite: sweet and full of flavour, enhanced by an ingredient that always makes them shine: almonds. (For a winter pudding that also makes use of this wonderful combination, turn to page 30.)

I think these baked apricots are nicest served oh-so-slightly warm, so you may want to factor this in to your timings.

10 fresh apricots, halved and the stones removed
20 amaretti biscuits
1 tablespoon brown sugar
Amaretto liqueur (about 20 teaspoons)

clotted cream, double cream or good-quality vanilla ice cream, to serve

Preheat the oven to 180°C/Gas Mark 4. Place the apricots, skin-side down, in a shallow baking dish. Then put the biscuits in a plastic bag and bash them vigorously with a rolling pin until they become coarse crumbs. Add the brown sugar, shake the whole lot up and then, using a teaspoon, pile some of the mixture in the holes and over the flat tops of each apricot half. Finish off by drizzling 1 teaspoon of the almond-scented Amaretto liqueur over the top of each. Bake in the oven for 25–30 minutes. Serve with good-quality cream or ice cream.

see page 16

Roast Pork with Crackling

Leg of Lamb with Cumin, Lemon and Mint see page 24

see page 36

Green Salad with Broad Beans and Goat's Cheese

Fresh Crab Cannelloni

see page 40

see page 64

Duck Legs with Port and Cranberries

Turnips and Leeks with Honey, Coriander and Soy see page 68

see page 93 Lavender Shortbread with Blackberries and Lemon Cream

Baked Peaches in Spiked Raspberry Purée

see page 98

Poultry and meat

I have to confess that my decision to not eat meat wasn't made out of principle. I think God made animals for all sorts of reasons, and one of them is for eating. Nevertheless, I have to admit that, as I write those words, I am struck by the shock factor that I am eating our four-legged friends: it does feel brutal to think of killing, say, a happy little lamb, cutting it up and sticking its leg in the oven. However, as I say, such kind and noble thoughts didn't inform my decision to turn veggie: it was just the meat at college tasted like dog food (not that I'd know) and it kind of put me off the carnivore thing altogether. And so it was that nearly two decades of abstinence began. My mother thought I had turned anorexic; my burger-loving then-boyfriend thought I had gone mad and, much later, my to-be-husband, when I met him, felt a touch disappointed.

However, I still cooked meat (surprisingly well, apparently) in my days of non-participation. Fast-forward to the present and I think poultry, game and meat are to die for (oh, sorry, it's the other way around). It was morning sickness in my second pregnancy that returned me to eating meat; endless sucking of lemon sherbets failed to rein in the nausea, but a bacon sandwich did the job in a jiffy. After that, I succumbed to chicken, rapidly moved on to game and then all my meaty barriers fell down rapidly. I like to think that, if he was still around, I'd have given my butcher grandfather a good boost to his business.

Dîner Français

Six of us for dinner, including a petite French girl and her husband. He currently works for a church but used to make violins for a living. Being good with his hands, he was tasked with putting in our £200 second-hand kitchen. 'It's only temporary, honest,' said the Vicar reassuringly, as a mismatched work surface was installed. Eighteen months on and I am still muddling along with too little storage space, an unreliable oven and frankly inadequate everything. Anyway, the violin-maker is not to blame for that, so tonight I made a meal in celebration of his lovely, diminutive French wife. For the main course, I plumped for poussin – in the chicken world it is small but perfectly formed, just like her.

CHICORY, PEAR AND PANCETTA SALAD

POUSSIN WITH BOURSIN AND BACON

LEEKY MASH

MAMAN'S TARTE AUX FRAISES

serves 6

Chicory, Pear and Pancetta Salad

Chicory is eaten rarely in this country, but it is beloved in France. Maybe it's because we British don't know what to do with it. That, or the fact that, when tasted by itself, it has a rather bitter flavour. In this salad, this bitterness is offset by the sweetness of the pear and the saltiness of the cheese. One guest (not the French one) finished his portion and said, in his broad Scottish tones, 'Well, I can't say I know what that was, but it was really very nice.'

2 heads of chicory
2 ripe pears
80g cubed pancetta
a lump of Pecorino or Parmesan
   cheese, for shaving

For the dressing:
4 tablespoons olive oil
1 tablespoon red wine vinegar
1½ teaspoons Dijon mustard
1 garlic clove, peeled and crushed
a pinch of caster sugar
2 teaspoons water

First, put all the ingredients for the dressing into a clean jar, put the lid on and shake it like crazy.

Next, make the salad. Take 6 side plates and place 3 leaves of chicory on each. Cut the rest of the leaves across into thin slices and set aside. Peel, quarter and core the pears and cut each quarter into 4 slices. In a frying pan, fry the pancetta without any oil and, once it's crispy and brown, remove from the pan and toss with the chopped chicory, the pear and two thirds of the dressing. Divide all this among the whole leaves on the plates and shave over some Pecorino or Parmesan, using your potato peeler. About 6 shavings per person should do it. Drizzle over a bit more dressing and serve.

Poussin with Boursin and Bacon

Years ago, a supermarket magazine did a version of this dish, but made with chicken breasts. I cooked it endlessly, and every time I did, the recipe was requested. So much so that I think I might have propagated it around the whole of London. I'd turn up at someone's house and there it was again; the failsafe dinner-party dish. When I enquired how it got there, the answer would always be that the recipe came from a friend … of a friend … of a friend …

Anyway, this is my updated version. Poussins are perfect dinner-party food, and if you have male guests they will love the idea of being presented with their very own dolly bird. I love the sort of cooking that involves a bit of prodding and poking and generally making a sticky mess; this recipe certainly offers all that. If you don't fancy doing the mucky stuff with your guests around, you could prepare it all up to the point at which it would go in the oven, either in the morning or the evening before your dinner party.

6 poussins
300g Boursin cheese
6 slices smoked streaky bacon
400ml white wine, possibly more

15g fresh tarragon leaves, chopped
juice of $\frac{1}{2}$ lemon
salt and pepper

Preheat the oven to 200°C/Gas Mark 6. Take your poussins and put them in a large, metal roasting tin. Using your fingers, separate the skin from the breast meat (it's fun, honest!); it's easiest if you just use your forefinger and slide it in carefully, as the last thing you want is to tear the skin. Now put aside half the Boursin to go in the sauce and, taking the other half, insert about 1 teaspoon of the cheese into each opened pouch. It's here that things will get a bit messy, but don't be tempted to lick your fingers as you are in contact with raw poultry and, as far as I know, no one has ever put Salmonella and pleasure in the same sentence. Push the rest of the Boursin for the poussins into each stomach cavity. Drape the bacon over the birds, pour the white wine into the tin and put it in the oven for about 50 minutes–1 hour.

After this time is up, stick a sharp knife into a nice fat part of the bird if you are worried about whether it's properly cooked through: the juices should run clear. If not, return them to the oven for another 5–7 minutes. When they are cooked, remove the poussins to a warm plate and add the rest of the Boursin, the tarragon, lemon juice and seasoning to the roasting tin, whisking everything together. Let it bubble away until it is reduced and well flavoured. It should not end up thin and watery (if it does, just cook it some more), but neither should it be too gloopy (if so, add more wine, or water). Serve the birds on top of the leeky mash (see recipe page 112), with some sauce spooned over the top and around.

serves 6   Poussin with Boursin and Bacon 111

Leeky Mash

I love leeks, perhaps because I'm Welsh, and I love mashed potato. Combine the two and it's pure Celtic comfort food.

1kg floury maincrop potatoes, such as King Edwards or Maris Piper
500g leeks, cleaned and very finely sliced

125g butter
200ml double cream
salt and pepper

Peel the potatoes and cut them into quarters. Put them in a pan of boiling salted water, bring back to the boil, cover and cook for 20–25 minutes or until soft. (Turn the heat down to medium if you don't want boiling water flooding out of the pan and onto your stove.)

Meanwhile, the leeks need to be slowly sweated in half the butter for 10–15 minutes; you are aiming for them to be softened, not browned. Just before the potatoes are ready, heat up the rest of the butter and the cream in a small pan. Drain the potatoes and tip them into a large bowl. Add the leeks, the hot butter and cream and lots of salt and pepper, and either mash heartily with a potato masher or, even better, whisk with an electric whisk. If you want you can make this before people arrive and either keep it warm over a pan of boiling water or (easier), for those of us who aren't microwave-shy, just pop it in there for about five minutes and give it a really good stir before serving.

serves 6

Maman's Tarte aux Fraises

Making pastry is something I try and avoid. My mother, whilst insisting 'there was no point in it', was so good at turning out the most perfect jam tart that I am loath to try and upstage her. As if I could. But here we go. Here is a strawberry tart that might give my mother a run for her money …

For the sweet pastry:
75g butter, at room temperature
75g caster sugar
150g plain flour
3 large egg yolks, beaten

For the filling:
250g mascarpone
1 tablespoon icing sugar
250g ripe strawberries, hulled and
   halved
2 tablespoons Bonne Maman jam
   (or any good-quality jam)

For the pastry blend the butter, sugar and flour in a food processor until the mixture resembles fine breadcrumbs. Beat the egg yolks into the mixture gradually, until the whole thing starts to turn into a doughy blob. Plop the doughy blob onto a lightly floured surface and knead it lightly for a minute or so until it is smooth and round. Wrap it in cling film and chill it in the fridge for 30 minutes or until you want to roll it out. When you are ready to bake, lightly grease a 20cm flan ring and preheat the oven to 190°C/Gas Mark 5. Place the flan ring on a baking tray and take the dough out of the fridge before kneading it for a minute to soften it up. Roll it out so that it is about 5cm bigger in diameter than the flan ring. Carefully place the rolled-out pastry into the ring, pressing it firmly into the sides. Trim off any extra pastry around the rim and prick the base lightly with a fork. Cover the pastry with greaseproof paper and pile in either baking beans or dried pulses, before chilling the flan ring in the fridge for at least 15 minutes. Once your pastry is nicely chilled, take it out of the fridge and pop the flan ring in the oven to bake for 15–20 minutes. Then take the flan tin out of the oven and remove the paper and beans before popping it back in the oven to cook for a further 5 minutes, or until the pastry has a pleasing golden hue. Remove the flan tin from the oven and allow the pastry to cool, after which you can remove the flan ring (but not the base) when you are brave enough to do so.

Meanwhile, to make the filling, beat together the mascarpone and icing sugar and pile it onto the base of the pastry. Arrange the strawberries, cut side down, on top of the unctuous creamy mixture and warm the jam over a low heat in a small saucepan until it is hot and liquidy. Brush the melted jam over the strawberries and then chill your beautiful confection for at least 20 minutes in the fridge, lest it all goes soggy.

A fruity feast

Four of us for dinner tonight and a big lump of unsmoked gammon sat in the fridge all day. I stared at it for quite a long time before deciding what to do with it – my thoughts drifting between that old-fashioned porky-pineapple combo and Nigella Lawson's ham cooked in Coca-Cola. I ended up putting the two ideas together: I braised the ham in Lilt (the pineapple and grapefruit fizzy drink), and picked up the grapefruit notes in a pink grapefruit salsa. Sounds totally crazy, I know, and I only confessed how I'd cooked the ham after all of it had been gobbled up. It's a dish that proves that, sometimes, in the kitchen at least, being a bit mad isn't necessarily a bad thing.

HONEYED HAM WITH PINK GRAPEFRUIT SALSA

FRIED POTATOES WITH SOURED CREAM AND CHIVES

GREEN SALAD (SEE PAGE 267)

BLACKBERRY AND BLUEBERRY ETON MESS

serves 4

Honeyed Ham with Pink Grapefruit Salsa

This ham would be fabulous cold as well as hot. I served it with fried potatoes to give a cheeky, yet dignified, nod to pub ham and chips. Incidentally, if you doubled or even tripled the quantities (upping the cooking times accordingly, of course), this whole meal would make a fabulous feast for a crowd. And it's easy to do, too.

1kg unsmoked gammon
700ml Lilt (not the diet version)
1 onion, peeled and quartered
2 tablespoons runny honey

For the salsa:
1 large pink grapefruit

½ red onion, peeled and finely
   chopped
2 tablespoons coriander, chopped
2 teaspoons olive oil
salt and pepper

Remove the gammon from the fridge about 20 minutes before you want to cook it. As it is unsmoked, it won't need soaking. Put it in a large pan with the Lilt and the onion and bring everything to the boil. Pop on the lid, reduce the heat so that the Lilt is just simmering, and cook for 1¼ hours. (Gammon takes 55 minutes per kg, plus 30 minutes.) As the ham (Nigella tells me that gammon becomes ham once it is cooked) nears the end of its cooking time, preheat the oven to 200°C/Gas Mark 6.

Meanwhile, prepare the salsa. Take a thin slice off the top and bottom of the grapefruit, then sit it on a board. Slice away all the skin and white pith to reveal the fruit. Then slice away the segments from between the pieces of membrane. Do this over a large bowl, as you want to keep all of the lovely juice. Combine the grapefruit with the onion and coriander, pour over the juice and olive oil and season. Stir it all together gently, and it's ready.

Once the ham is cooked, take it out of its fruity bath and pop it in a roasting tin. Drizzle the honey over the skin of the meat and put the tin in the oven for around 10 minutes. Carve the ham into slices and serve with a helping of salsa on the side, the fried potatoes and their soured cream dressing (see recipe on page 118) and an unfussy green salad.

Fried Potatoes with Soured Cream and Chives

500g maincrop potatoes, such as
    King Edwards or Maris Piper
2 tablespoons olive oil
salt and pepper

275ml soured cream
1 garlic clove, peeled and crushed
2 tablespoons chives, finely
    chopped

Wash the potatoes and slice them into rounds that are around 5mm thick.
Put them in a large pan of boiling salted water and parboil them for around
7 minutes, then drain. (This can be done any time during the cooking of the
ham.) About 15 minutes before you are ready to serve the gammon, heat the
oil in a frying pan and toss in the potatoes, coating them evenly with the oil.
Don't move them around too much – you want each side of the potato to
turn a rich, golden-brown colour. When they've reached this stage, season
them well. You can drain them on kitchen paper if you think they need it, but
they are probably fine as they are.

At some point while the potatoes are cooking, stir together the soured cream,
garlic, chives and a little seasoning in a bowl and put it on the table for
people to smear liberally over their potatoes, if they wish.

Blackberry and Blueberry Eton Mess

After experimenting with the ham, I plumped for something safer for pudding. Nevertheless, it was a classic with a twist. (New recipes are so often about re-inventing the wheel – there being only so many ingredients and flavour combinations in the world.) This is my version of the well-loved dessert, Eton Mess, which is perfect for when you've spotted some really good blackberries, or even picked them. Unless I've got some unused egg whites knocking around, I don't always make my own meringues for this. I find the meringue nests made by Marks & Spencer, and also Walkers, have a pleasing enough chewiness to them, which is what I think you're really after when it comes to meringues.

568ml double cream
finely grated zest of 1 lemon
300g blackberries
1 tablespoon icing sugar

1 tablespoon crème de mûre
 (blackberry liqueur) (optional)
150g blueberries
8 meringues, around 250g in total,
 broken up into small pieces

Put the cream into a mixing bowl and whip it to the floppy stage – you don't want it to be too stiff. Add the lemon zest to the cream.

Take half of the blackberries and whizz them in a blender with the icing sugar and the crème de mûre, if using. Remove the pips by pushing the purée through a sieve into a bowl. Put the rest of the blackberries in a big bowl with the blueberries, halving any whole blackberries if they are firm enough to cope with it. All this can be done in advance.

serves 4   Blackberry and Blueberry Eton Mess   119

When you are ready to serve, stir together the cream and the broken-up meringues. Finally, swirl in the purée, being careful not to stir it all in until it disappears because you want to retain a blackberry ripple effect. Serve straight away.

A welcoming dinner

It's a cold evening in October: time to batten down the hatches with friends who are the equivalent of well-loved old socks. They've just returned to London after a few years of living in Manhattan. As we catch up and they tell us tales of New York glamour, constant eating out and parties with George Clooney, somehow it feels right to be sitting there with them, eating steaming plates of unpretentious, rustic grub. Thanks for shanks, I say.

LAMB SHANKS BRAISED IN RED WINE

MUSTARD MASH (SEE PAGE 18)

FLAGEOLET BEANS WITH GARLIC

STICKY BREAD AND BUTTER PUDDING

serves 4

Lamb Shanks Braised in Red Wine

The Chinese say that good food is as much about the variety of textures as it is about taste. Here, I try to take this on board, British-style. This dish combines hearty meat with pillow-soft mash and grainy, earthy beans. A winning combination that, I think, proves the Chinese right.

4 lamb shanks

3 tablespoons seasoned flour

3 tablespoons oil

2 carrots, peeled and cut across into 2cm chunks

2 onions, peeled and sliced

2 garlic cloves, peeled and crushed

4 medium tomatoes, each cut into 8

500ml gutsy red wine

250ml lamb stock (fresh, or use a good-quality liquid bouillon)

1 tablespoon herbes de Provence

4 sprigs of rosemary, leaves removed

4 anchovy fillets in olive oil, drained and chopped

1 tablespoon ready-made redcurrant jelly

salt and pepper

Toss the shanks in the seasoned flour to coat, then heat 2 tablespoons of the oil in a large flameproof pan that the meat and vegetables will fit into comfortably. Brown the shanks in the oil until they are a lovely burnished bronze then remove to a plate.

Add the last tablespoon of oil to the pan and throw in the carrots, onions and garlic. Make sure the heat isn't too high now, as you don't want the vegetables to turn the same colour as the meat: you want soft, but not brown. Cook for about 5 minutes, then stir in the tomatoes, put the shanks back in the pot, add the wine and bring it to the boil. Pour in the stock and add the herbs. Herbes de Provence are a delightful mixture of herbs which traditionally contain lavender. The ones I use at the moment were bought in France, but I have also seen them in a shop in Bloomsbury, but that's a fat lot of use to you if you live in a small village near Scarborough. Add all the other ingredients and season, but don't add too much salt because whilst the anchovies won't impart a fishy flavour, they will add saltiness. Now slap a lid on the pan and turn the heat right down low. You could also, if it's easier, cook this dish in the oven at 160°C/Gas Mark 3.

Have a look after 2 hours, but it may take longer for the meat to reach the point of desired tenderness: that is, almost falling off the bone. Taste for seasoning and serve the lamb on the mashed potato, sauce spooned over the top, with the beans to one side.

Flageolet Beans with Garlic

1 x 400g tin flageolet beans (or butter beans)
2 tablespoons olive oil

2 garlic cloves, peeled and crushed
salt and pepper

Pour the beans into a sieve and rinse them under the cold tap. Now put them in a pan with the oil and garlic to heat through gently. I gave them a gentle mash with a fork from time to time to give the beans a varied texture. Season and serve.

Sticky Bread and Butter Pudding

I have a very hazy memory of eating syrup sandwiches as a child. Not very healthy, I know, but maybe we had just run out of honey. This bread and butter pudding uses syrup instead of sugar and thus gains a caramel richness. I love bread and butter pudding with a passion, and this one really hit the spot on a cold night. This dessert serves six, so there's enough for seconds or leftovers.

6–7 thin slices (about 5mm) of good white bread cut from a very fresh tin loaf, buttered, crusts removed and cut into quarters
60g raisins
4 tablespoons golden syrup, plus 2 tablespoons extra for glazing the top

3 medium eggs
1 egg yolk
300ml full-fat milk
250ml double cream

Place half of the pieces of buttered bread in overlapping rows in a shallow, oblong or oval, 2-litre baking dish.

Sprinkle half the raisins on top of the bread, then drizzle over 2 tablespoons of the golden syrup. My then 4-year-old got involved in this process with hands-on (or should I say hands-in) enthusiasm, underlining for me that I had given the pudding exactly the right name. Repeat the same process with the remaining ingredients, finishing with syrup.

Beat together the eggs, egg yolk, milk and cream and pour it over the pudding. Using a palette knife, push the bread down into the liquid, then leave the dish on the side for around 30 minutes for the bread to really soak up its sweetened dairy drink. Preheat the oven to 190°C/Gas Mark 5. Put the baking dish in a *bain-marie* (which simply means you put it in a bigger dish with hot, not boiling, water coming to about halfway up the sides of the baking dish containing the pudding), and bake it in the oven for 25–30 minutes, by which time the custard should be softly set and the top golden.

Now drizzle over the extra 2 tablespoons of golden syrup and place the dish under a hot grill. Don't forget about it: cook it carefully for 30 seconds or so until it is nicely caramelised. You want the pudding to be sweetly glazed, not bitterly burnt. Serve with some good-quality vanilla ice cream.

A winter's tail

Oh dear. I've finally had to face up to it: winter is really here. Everyone rushes grimly from A to B, trying to limit their time spent in the cold, and hats, gloves and scarves are simply *de rigueur*.

Tonight I decide to banish the blues and chase the chills with a comforting stew and an indulgent pudding. To start, it's oxtail – a cut many people are suspicious of. I can kind of understand it: raw oxtail looks far from appetising, with its thick, milky-white central bone, and cows' tails don't appear to be the most obvious thing in the world to eat. So when I announced to my guests that it was oxtail on the menu, I was far from surprised to pick up a sense of forced bravado. I could see, behind the carefully arranged faces and polite smiles, a deep sense of unease.

However, I knew my menu instincts were right: the guests were all feisty types, full of character, and the food needed to be gutsy enough to stand up to them. And indeed it did. The punchy, yet tender, meat was the perfect backdrop to their fond but lively banter. Everyone was won round and all went home happy and replete, tails wagging.

OXTAIL IN PORTER

MASH (SEE LEEKY MASH ON PAGE 112)

WHITE CHOCOLATE AND AMARETTO ICE CREAM

Oxtail in Porter

Whilst oxtail is rich, it's not cloyingly so. And you don't have to be rich to buy it, either.

I used porter (a dark beer a little like stout) in this stew because it's full-flavoured and powerful, and so can happily and confidently get cosy with the gutsy meat.

3 tablespoons plain flour
2 teaspoons English mustard
 powder
salt and pepper
2kg oxtail, cut into 5cm-thick
 pieces
4 tablespoons sunflower oil
1 leek, cleaned and cut into 1cm
 chunks

2 carrots, peeled and cut into 1cm
 chunks
2 onions, peeled and thickly sliced
2 celery sticks, thinly sliced
3 garlic cloves, peeled and crushed
500ml porter
200ml beef stock (fresh, or use a
 good-quality liquid bouillon)
6 sprigs of thyme

You will need a large flameproof casserole dish for this. As ever, I used my cauldron that can go in the oven as well as on the stove. Preheat the oven to 150°C/Gas Mark 2. This is an ideal dish to make ahead – either to reheat and eat on the next day or so or to freeze for another time – as stews benefit from a bit of time to themselves before eating, so that the various components and flavours get the chance to get together and form a team.

Chuck the flour in a large bowl and stir in the mustard powder and plenty of seasoning. Add the pieces of oxtail and coat them evenly with the flour. Pour 3 tablespoons of the oil into your casserole or pan and set the heat to high. Brown the meat in the oil, in batches if necessary, and then, once it's got a nice colour, remove and put it on a couple of plates. Add another tablespoon of oil to the pan, turn the heat down to medium, add the vegetables and garlic and fry for 5–6 minutes or until softened, but not brown. Re-introduce the meat to the pan, add the porter and let it come to the boil and bubble away for a few minutes. Add the stock, thyme and a little seasoning, slip on a lid and put it in the oven. It can stay there for 2–3 hours quite happily.

Once the meat is tender, take out the casserole, test for seasoning, and leave to cool. The stew can either go in the fridge for the next day, or the freezer for a rainy one. Just remember that oxtail is quite fatty, but this will all conveniently set in a layer on the top of the stew whilst it's in the fridge. Remove all the fat and then reheat the stew – this should take about 15 minutes on the hob. However, if you are serving it straight away, skim off the excess fat from the surface with a spoon.

I served my stew on buttery creamy mash. There are enough fiddled about mash recipes in this book without my telling you how to make the plain stuff. If in doubt, just use the recipe for leeky mash on page 112, replacing the leeks with the same quantity of potatoes.

serves 6

White Chocolate and Amaretto Ice Cream

This pudding makes a wonderful contrast to the gutsy stew, being light, but creamily decadent. When the Vicar has taken weddings we have usually had the happy couple over for supper at some point before the big day. It was on one such evening that the bride-to-be mentioned this recipe that her mother had given her. We were eating a pudding of my own creation at the time, but I have to say that when I made her mother's offering some time later, it put my own handiwork in the shade. I served this recently to my brother, an ice cream aficionado, and its creamy perfection generated just two words: 'Oh yes.'

When served as dessert after the stew, this ice cream makes for a very carefree evening for the cook, as both are make-ahead dishes.

300g good-quality white chocolate, broken into squares

4 tablespoons full-fat milk

5 tablespoons Amaretto di Saronno liqueur

300ml double cream

2 large fresh eggs, separated

Around $1/4$ of a packet of amaretti biscuits

First, line a 1kg loaf tin with cling film. Then put the chocolate into a small pan with the milk and leave it to melt on a very low heat. Once it's all glossy and lick-able, remove it from the hob and pour into a bowl. Add the liqueur, mix together and allow to cool. Lightly whip the cream. Beat the egg yolks into the cooled chocolate mixture and then gently fold in the cream. With clean dry whisks, whisk the egg whites until stiff in a large clean bowl and then fold gently into the chocolate mixture.

Put the amaretti biscuits into a plastic bag and bash vigorously with a heavy rolling pin, or something similar, to make coarse crumbs. Sprinkle some of the crumbs over the base of the loaf tin to make a 5mm-thick layer. Spoon half of the ice cream mixture over the biscuits, top with another layer of biscuits, then finish off with the rest of the soon-to-be ice cream. Cover with clingfilm and freeze for at least 5 hours or until firm. Serve cut into dreamy slices.

Vegetarian

After all my enthusiasm for meat, please don't think I'm anti-vegetarian. I'm not. Despite any playful comments, I respect those who feel that eating meat is against their conscience and so don't do it. As I say, my reason for depriving myself of meat was far less worthy – I just thought I didn't like it. Now that I've discovered I do, I can't get enough of it and I have spent the last three and a half years playing carnivore catch-up. I fear this fact has somewhat swayed the balance of recipes in this book, so I beg forgiveness from those keen to cook vegetarian.

As someone who has had to watch the pennies, I feel doubly ashamed about my paltry veggie offerings, as good meat is expensive, as is fish. Blame the Vicar, I say. Even when I was a staunch vegetarian, he never budged. For him, a meal without meat is as good as a church without people or tonic without gin. Vegetables, he says, are just the colourful stuff on the side; they do not a real meal make.

Autumn on a plate

It's the end of October, with Halloween tomorrow and a weekend of bonfires to come. I'm not a great fan of Halloween, but I do like this season, food-wise. Suddenly pumpkins are rife outside my greengrocer's, their orange coats bringing a glow to grey days. Once lugged home, hollowed out and filled with a candle, they lend a comforting magic to my kitchen that draws the children to the table without struggle or fight.

However, when it comes to actually cooking pumpkins and all the other squashes, it has to be said that they are a devil to prepare. Uncooked, their flesh is very dense and hard to cut through, and they also have very thick skins that are a pain to cut off. What is imperative, here, is that you use a very, very sharp knife. If you have to run out and buy a knife sharpener, then so be it. Even armed with such an implement, preparing squashes is no pleasant walk in the park, but try and do the job with a blunt knife and it's a total nightmare: it feels like you have no control over your blade whatsoever (which you haven't).

If the work involved has you hissing with frustration, be assured that it'll all be worth it. I always think of butternut squash as treasure chests: they are so infuriatingly difficult to prise open, but once you have done so and have cooked them you are rewarded with the sweetest, pure gold that richly satisfies. Perfect fodder for a cold grey day.

This butternut squash and porcini risotto is one that bursts with the best of autumn. The cooked flesh of the squash is beautiful here, releasing a warm, uncloying sweetness that is the perfect complement to the woody earthiness of the porcini. After that, there's a pudding in honour of the pear.

For me, pears spell autumn: this mellow season is their time, and whilst summer shouts berries and winter, tangerines, autumn is when we are called to celebrate the pear's sweetly scented gentleness.

BUTTERNUT SQUASH AND PORCINI RISOTTO

PEAR CHOCOLATE BETTY

serves 4   Dinner for Friends   133

Butternut Squash and Porcini Risotto

Incidentally, I served this dish to rabid carnivores and it went down a storm.

1 squash (preferably a butternut with a long neck, as this part contains most flesh)
4 tablespoons olive oil
2 shallots, peeled and finely chopped
20g dried porcini mushrooms, soaked in 500ml boiling water

300g risotto rice, such as Arborio or Canaroli
150ml white wine
75g soft goat's cheese (Rosary would be perfect)
2 tablespoons Grana Padano or Parmesan cheese, finely grated
salt and pepper

This dish takes time, albeit in a relatively undemanding way, so it's one to make when you fancy an evening of idle, soothing stirring whilst your guests sit around in the kitchen and chat. In other words, this isn't a recipe to choose if you are having over the scary boss whom you'd prefer not to see you cook.

Peel and core the squash and then cut it into 1cm pieces. Heat the oil in a large pan; add the squash and start cooking with the lid off the pan, stirring occasionally so the squash doesn't stick. After 20 minutes, add the shallots and allow them to soften. Place the lid on the pan, make sure the heat is low, and let it cook gently until the hour is up, giving it a stir now and again. Taste a bit of the squash – it should be starting to release its sweetness, and will continue to do so as the risotto comes together. The alternative way of dealing with the squash could be to halve it lengthways, whilst it is still raw and in its skin, and put it in a roasting tin in an oven set at 200°C/Gas Mark 6 for 1 hour. After that, scrape out and discard the seeds, then spoon out the soft flesh. Pan fry the shallots in some oil and stir both the shallots and squash into the finished risotto.

However, I went for the more hands-on approach and chose to have the squash involved in the stovetop cooking process from the start. Whichever way you choose, whilst the squash is cooking, line a sieve with 2 pieces of kitchen paper and put it over a jug, then tip the soaked porcini mushrooms into the sieve to drain and so remove any grit that is in the water. Squeeze the mushrooms over the sieve to remove as much liquid from them as possible. Check how much mushroom stock is left: some may have been swallowed up by the greedy little fungi (and the kitchen paper!) If so, make the stock back up to 500ml again by adding just boiled water, chicken stock, or, as I did, some water saved from boiling vegetables. Put whatever liquid you are using into a pan on the hob and heat until bubbling.

Chop the porcini finely – it is easier, to be honest, to snip them with scissors, as they are slippery little things. Add the rice to the squash in the pan and stir to get everything acquainted. Add the porcini, stir, and then pour in the wine. Let this bubble away until it has almost vanished and then add a ladleful of hot stock. Stir until this has absorbed and keep doing this, patiently stirring and, if you like, chatting in a 'Look at me, I'm so relaxed in the kitchen', nonchalant sort of way to your admiring guests for 20–25 minutes. Keep tasting the rice as the stock stash depletes. You are aiming to get rid of any hard bite and instead get the rice to the point of gooey creaminess. By now the butternut will be all squelchy and sticky and oozing around in the rice. Finish the risotto by adding the goat's cheese, which adds a hint of zestiness, and the Grana Padano or Parmesan, for its cheesy bite. Season well and serve in warm bowls, preferably on a cold autumn evening.

Pear Chocolate Betty

This is my take on Nigel Slater's Apple Betty. I initially made it as I liked the idea of offering people a pudding called 'Betty', and indeed my guests welcomed her with joy and expressed huge fondness for this warm, consoling addition to our table. I swapped pears for apples as I adore the classic pear and chocolate combination. I also decreased the amount of sugar as, unlike Nigel's Bramleys, the pears exude their own sweetness.

1kg pears, peeled, quartered and
   cored
30g butter
125g soft white breadcrumbs
75g light soft brown sugar

100g good-quality dark chocolate,
   chopped
75g butter, melted
3 tablespoons golden syrup

Preheat the oven to 190°C/Gas Mark 5. Cut the pears into large chunks and put them in a pan with the butter. Add a couple of tablespoons of water and allow them to soften slightly over a medium heat, shaking them around in the pan frequently. How long this takes depends on the ripeness of your pears – mine took about 10 minutes. When they are soft and still holding their shape, but not soggy, tip them into a 1.5-litre, shallow baking dish.

For the topping, mix the breadcrumbs, sugar and chocolate together and scatter it over the pears. Now add the melted butter to the golden syrup in a pan and heat until blended, then pour the mixture carefully over the crumbs, taking care to cover all areas. Bake for 35 minutes, by which time the topping should be gooey, yet crisp and deliciously golden.

A cosy fondue party

Tonight, four to feed, and despite its connotations of 70s' kaftans, I plan a
fondue in which to dip roasted autumn squashes. For moments when the rich
cheesiness gets too much, there'll also be a hot and spicy tomato sauce on the
table. And there'll be good bread, too – pumpkin bread, in fact.

People often feel a bit heavy-stomached after a fondue, and the squash and
the potatoes are pretty filling, too, so I would just offer a platter of fresh fruit
for pudding. Include some beautiful little exotic numbers, such as physalis,
passion fruit and lychees, to make your no-work offerings look a bit special.

COMTÉ CHEESE FONDUE WITH ROASTED SQUASHES

RICH TOMATO SAUCE WITH HARISSA (SEE PAGE 303)

PLATTER OF FRESH FRUIT

Comté Cheese Fondue with Roasted Squashes

250g Comté cheese (a type of Gruyère, or just use Gruyère)

250g Emmental cheese

1 garlic clove, halved

350ml white wine

2 teaspoons cornflour

4 tablespoons cold water or kirsch

pepper

Vegetables for dipping:

1 small pumpkin

1 medium butternut squash

1 sweet potato (I know it's not a squash, but it feels right to include it)

2 tablespoons olive oil

salt and pepper

First, prepare the vegetables for dipping. Take a potato peeler and patiently remove the skins from all the vegetables. Now de-seed the pumpkin and the butternut squash and cut all the vegetables into chunks of about 2cm square. Put them in a roasting tin and into a hot oven that has been preheated to 220°C/Gas Mark 7. They need to roast for about 45 minutes–1 hour and you want them to emerge looking brown at the edges and with a hint of toffee about them. Incidentally, if there are any left over after the meal, stick them in a pan and blend them with enough water to make a soup that just asks to be accompanied by good bread and a few nice cheeses.

After the vegetables have been in the oven for about 20 minutes, prepare the fondue. I confess that when I made mine I felt quite nostalgic. It brought back memories, not of the 70s, but of the early 90s and a rather strange party in a wine bar in Earls Court with over-enthusiastic accordion players … but that's another story. Anyway, grate the cheeses, trying not to scoff them as you do so, and rub the halved clove of garlic around the inside of the pan in which you are going to cook the fondue. (A sturdy, heavy-based one is best.) Now pour in the wine and bring to the boil. Turn the heat down low and add the grated cheese, stirring all the time until is has melted and is gently bubbling. Mix the cornflour with the kirsch or water, stir into the fondue and add some seasoning. When everything looks 'together' serve it – preferably over a burner so you don't end up with stringy cheese or have to keep going back to the stove. Have prongs at the ready and Barry White on a loop.

If you want to serve the tomato sauce, too, see page 303 for the recipe. Just halve the quantities and save the rest as a pasta sauce.

Vegetarian goes posh

So often we think of vegetarian food as earthy fare; after all, lentils and tofu aren't really the heights of haute cuisine, are they? However, this menu is proof that meat-free food can 'put on the Ritz'. Soufflés are always glamorous, and this one, with its delicious base of wild mushrooms and its fresh, yet creamy, cloud-like top, is no exception. As for the cake, it is lighter than the word 'cake' would suggest, and as there's enough for eight, you might have some left over to have with your coffee the next day – if your guests don't scoff the lot.

WILD MUSHROOM AND GOAT'S CHEESE SOUFFLÉ

LAMB'S LETTUCE AND WALNUT SALAD

ALMOND CAKE WITH POACHED DAMSONS

Wild Mushroom and Goat's Cheese Soufflé

For the wild mushroom mixture:
40g butter
2 teaspoons olive oil
2 shallots, peeled, halved and thinly
    sliced
2 garlic cloves, peeled and thinly
    sliced
25g dried porcini mushrooms,
    soaked in 300ml boiling water
250g fresh wild mushrooms, cleaned
    and sliced
1–2 teaspoons fresh thyme leaves

For the soufflé:
1 small onion, peeled and halved
3 cloves

300ml full-fat milk
300ml double cream
1 bay leaf
$^1\!/_2$ teaspoon black peppercorns
75g butter
40g plain flour
5 large eggs, separated
leaves from 2 large sprigs of thyme,
    plus extra to garnish
150g soft fresh goat's cheese (such
    as Rosary, Welsh Pant-Ysgawn or
    French Crotin de Chavignol),
    crumbled
25g Parmesan cheese, finely grated
$^1\!/_4$ teaspoon cayenne pepper
salt and pepper

First, relax. I know the thought of making a soufflé may well have you fleeing the kitchen in panic, but it really isn't that scary, I promise, and this one is particularly easy. Because it is poured into a shallow, ovenproof dish, there's not so much of a worry about whether it will rise theatrically over the top of the soufflé dish or just fall flat: in a shallow dish it will at least look puffy. So do try and enjoy yourself while you're cooking, and just look forward to what will be a bountiful meal.

Start making the sauce that will end up being the goat's cheese soufflé. Stud the onion with the cloves and put it into a small pan with the milk, cream, bay leaf and peppercorns. Bring to the boil, then set aside for 20 minutes to allow the flavours to blend together. Then strain the milk through a sieve into a bowl, discarding the onion and any other bits. Melt the butter in a non-stick pan, add the flour and cook over a medium heat for 1 minute to cook out the flour. Gradually beat in the infused milk and bring to the boil, stirring, then leave to simmer very gently over a very low heat for 10 minutes, giving it a stir every now and then. Pour the mixture into a mixing bowl and leave to cool slightly. Preheat the oven now to 200°C/Gas Mark 6.

Next, it's time for the wild mushroom mixture. Heat the butter and the oil in a deep frying pan and, when it's bubbling, add the shallots and garlic and cook gently until soft. Drain the porcini, squeezing out any excess water. Chop them up finely and add them to the pan. Cook them for a few minutes before adding the wild mushrooms and thyme leaves. Keeping the heat high, allow the mushrooms to soften for a couple of minutes until soft, but stop cooking before the juices start to seep out. Chuck the whole lot into the bottom of a lightly buttered, shallow, oval ovenproof dish measuring 30cm x 18cm and about 5cm deep.

Return to the soufflé now. Separate the eggs into two bowls, putting the whites into a large mixing bowl. Mix the egg yolks into the cooled sauce, then stir in half the thyme leaves, the crumbled goat's cheese, the grated Parmesan, cayenne pepper, ¾ teaspoon of salt and some black pepper. Now whisk the egg whites until they stand in soft peaks and then gently fold them into the cheesy mixture. Pour the whole lot over the mushrooms, sprinkle with the remaining thyme leaves and bake on the middle shelf of the oven for 30 minutes or until the top is puffed up and golden but the centre still soft and creamy. Garnish with a few fresh thyme leaves and serve with the salad.

Lamb's Lettuce and Walnut Salad

This salad is perfect with the soufflé: the soft flavour of the lamb's lettuce really complements the cheesy goo and woodland mushrooms. Walnuts and goat's cheese should get married.

1 garlic clove
200g lamb's lettuce
2 tablespoons walnuts, preferably fresh

For the dressing:
2 tablespoons olive oil
1 tablespoon walnut oil
1 tablespoon red wine vinegar
1 teaspoon Dijon mustard
salt and pepper

Cut the garlic in half and rub the cut end around the inside of the bowl in which you will serve the salad, then toss in the lettuce and the walnuts. In a separate bowl, whisk together all the dressing ingredients. Toss the salad with enough of the dressing to coat the leaves, and you're ready to serve.

Almond Cake with Poached Damsons

You'll have to be quick to pick up some damsons, as their season is so short. If you fail, then just use plums instead.

For the cake:
100g butter, plus extra for greasing
150g caster sugar, plus extra for
    dusting
3 large eggs
75g ground almonds
40g plain flour
2–3 drops of almond extract
    (optional)

cream (double or single), to serve
    (optional)

For the poached damsons:
120ml red wine or port
450g damsons or plums
4 tablespoons good redcurrant jelly
finely grated zest and juice of
    1 orange

First, poach the damsons. Pour the wine or port into a pan just large enough to take the damsons or plums, and boil until reduced by half. Add the redcurrant jelly and stir gently until it has dissolved, then add the orange zest and juice. Halve and stone the plums (damsons will have to remain whole with their stones intact), and place them in the pan with their cut sides down into the red wine/port syrup. Bring the syrup to the boil, let it bubble up over the fruit, then lower the heat and leave the fruit to poach gently until it is tender. How long this takes depends on the ripeness of the fruit – give them about 10 minutes, but check and don't let them disintegrate. Spoon the poached fruit and syrup into a bowl and leave to cool.

For the cake, grease and flour an 18cm loose-bottomed, deep, straight-sided sandwich tin and line the base with greaseproof paper. Preheat the oven to 180°C/Gas Mark 4. Cream the butter in a bowl and then beat in the sugar, 1 tablespoon at a time, until the mixture is light and fluffy. Beat in the eggs one at a time, beating in one-third of the almonds with each egg. Gently fold in the flour and the almond extract, if using. Spoon the mixture into the prepared tin and lightly level out the top. Bake for 45–50 minutes or until the cake has shrunk away from the sides of the tin slightly and a skewer inserted into the centre of the cake comes out clean.

Turn the cake out onto a cooling rack that has a clean tea towel over it. (I know that sounds odd, but it stops the rack marking the delicate surface of the cake.) Remove the base of the tin and the lining paper. Cover the cake with a flat serving plate and carefully turn it over onto it. Dust the top of the cake with a little caster sugar and serve warm with the plum or damson compôte and some cream, if you wish.

The very word 'supper' has a cosy feel to it: it conjures up feelings of unpretentious, homely warmth. There is none of the stiff nervousness of dinner; the mood is idle, sloppy even. Plates don't have to match, knives are optional, and elbows have a place on the table. As for the food, tasty as it is, it's not there to show off or shout, but rather to provide succour and strength at the end of a busy day. When all this is shared with people you care about, supper becomes something that is about openness, acceptance and warmth. It not only gives you the chance to talk away lingering stresses or share silly tales, but it also allows you to tuck into good food with all your oft-hidden bad table manners on display, safe in the knowledge that they don't matter: you are loved.

Indeed, to verge on the confessional, whilst I love putting on a show for a beautiful dinner, the midweek supper shared with an old, forgiving friend is something very dear to my heart. The Vicar and I have enjoyed some of our sweetest times when we have had a lurking free evening and have chatted at the kitchen table, comforting ourselves with whatever it is we've made to eat. I say we, but actually the Vicar plays no part in the cooking bit. It is not that he's lazy; it's just that he knows that cooking makes me so happy – and it makes him equally happy to let me get on with it and enjoy whatever it is I dish up.

All the recipes in this chapter are intended to be knocked up on the night. None is difficult or time-consuming, but all are just what you are after at the end of a hard day: good, nutritious, tasty grub that hasn't cost an arm and a leg. All too many of us these days eschew any real cooking for some shop-bought packet that is usually eaten inattentively in front of the box. I'm not saying it's wrong to do this once in a while, but it's obvious that, long-term,

Weekday Suppers

this is a more expensive, not to mention unhealthy, way of living. Not only that, but by doing this we miss out on the satisfying joy of combining good ingredients, however simply, and the comparable pleasure that comes about when different people sit round a table and really talk. In cooking, ingredients usually need other ingredients to bring out their best side and reveal what they have to offer. The same is often true of us. So, I dare you, switch off that telly and get in the kitchen. Even my mother, who lives alone, can be found of an evening exploring what food goes with what and often phones up to describe the results of her happy experiments, as well as talk about lots of other stuff, too.

So feel free to cook your midweek suppers following a whim or what you have available in your fridge and cupboards; however, if you do want some guidance, I humbly offer here some recipe suggestions that are easy and quick to cook. Serve them on their own or just accompany them with whatever salad or vegetables need eating up. This isn't meant to be elegant food; just stuff to get you fed, albeit rather well.

Monday-night Risotto

We had a chicken for Sunday lunch, and I prolonged the fowl experience by making a stock with the carcass on Sunday afternoon. I did it extremely half-heartedly, slapdash girl that I am. This time I omitted any vegetables and just threw some cold water over the skeleton in the pan. Once the water was boiling, I left it on a very gentle simmer for 2 hours, filling the downstairs with smells of fuggy warmth. After that I strained it and put it to chill. (If you want a recipe for a more carefully made stock, not that it's in any way difficult, turn to page 224.) The next evening, with the stock and some leftover chicken, the Monday-night risotto was soothingly wonderful; its flavour rich, yet kind. If any dish could make you feel that the world is a safe place, this is the one.

Please don't be put off by the whole stirring thing that's part and parcel of making a risotto: think of it as time out, remedial, even. As someone who tries to do lots of things all at once and ends up doing them all pretty badly, a risotto in the pan forces me to focus and, well, calm down and shut up. Now I realise why the Vicar is quite so fond of this dish …

serves 4

1.2 litres hot chicken stock (fresh, or use a good-quality liquid bouillon – please don't make this if you don't have any of the real stuff, a stock cube really will not do)

60g butter

1 small onion, peeled and finely chopped

1 leek, cleaned and finely chopped

300g risotto rice, such as Arborio or Canaroli

150ml white wine

100g leftover chicken in various-sized chunks, slices and slithers, skin removed

juice of $\frac{1}{2}$ lemon

1 tablespoon double cream

3 tablespoons Parmesan cheese, grated

salt and pepper

Put the stock into a large pan, bring to a simmer and keep hot over a low heat. In another large pan, melt half the butter and stir in the onion. After about a minute, add the leek and soften on a gentle heat for about 5 minutes. Add the rice and stir to coat each grain with the buttery vegetable goo. Pour in the wine, and once reduced (that means you let it bubble away until it evaporates), add the hot stock, ladle by ladle. Allow each ladle's worth to become absorbed before you add the next, stirring all the time in a spirit of monastic calm. All this will go on for 20–25 minutes, so, to aid quiet reflection, you may want to have a little glass of the wine on the side for restorative sipping. Once the rice is soft and lovely, add the chicken and stir until hot, then add the rest of the ingredients, the remaining butter going in last. Season with salt and pepper, serve on warm plates, and enjoy this risotto's kindly caress.

Courgette, Mint and Pea Risotto

Another risotto, this time for those for whom chicken stock is a no-no. When I was a vegetarian I used to intensely dislike all vegetarian 'meat substitutes' and the oh-so-worthy 70s hotpot fests that made me feel I ought to be dressed in sackcloth and sandals. For me, this courgette risotto would have been perfect vegetarian fare. Making use of seasonal vegetables and adding a bit of alchemy to make them shine, in this case the milky saltiness of the feta and freshness of the mint, is what loving, imaginative cooking is all about – vegetarian or not. I can't claim that this is one I made earlier, as this recipe is from my dear friend, Clara.

4 tablespoons olive oil, plus extra to serve

1.3kg courgettes, cut into 2cm pieces (Clara used a mixture of baby courgettes, white and yellow courgettes and ordinary green ones, but use whatever is available)

salt and pepper

6 shallots, peeled and finely diced (to make them easier to peel, pour boiling water over them for 30 seconds or so)

1.5 litres vegetable stock (i.e. vegetable cooking water, see page 223, or use a good-quality liquid bouillon)

450g risotto rice, such as Arborio or Canaroli

300ml white wine

300g frozen peas (defrosted)

400g feta, cut into small cubes

large handful of mint leaves, chiffonaded (in layman's terms, very finely shredded. Can't you tell the lovely Clara trained at Leith's Cookery School?) plus a few whole leaves, to garnish

serves 6

Heat 2 tablespoons of the oil in a large frying pan, then add the courgettes and a sprinkling of salt. Fry gently until they begin to soften – about 3–4 minutes – then remove and set aside.

Heat the rest of the oil in a large pan and add the shallots. If you wish, cover the shallots with a circle of damp greaseproof paper cut out to the same size as the pan – this should ensure they soften slowly without browning. Leave on a very low heat for 5–6 minutes or until they are translucent and tender. Meanwhile, heat up the vegetable stock in another pan until it is gently bubbling away. When the shallots have softened, add the rice and stir it to coat each grain with the oil and juicy onions. After a minute, add the wine and stir until it is more or less absorbed and the 'alcoholic' smell has gone from the pan. Now add the hot stock, ladle by ladle, adding more when the previous ladleful has been almost completely absorbed. Stir constantly if you can, but don't panic if you have to pop away for a minute – just don't go too far. When most of the stock has been added, which should take around 20–25 minutes, stir in the peas. By now the rice should be soft and creamy and you can remove it from the heat and stir in the feta and the mint.

Season with salt and pepper, put a lid on the pan and leave for 2 minutes (this may be a good opportunity to dress a salad/get people to the table/pour another glass of wine). Serve in warm bowls garnished with whole mint leaves and drizzled with olive oil. Then give a toast to Clara.

Kitchen Carbonara

With the wine and cream and smoked salmon, you could mistake this dish for elegant. Don't worry, though, once you both start slurping that pasta down, that word is the last one that will spring to mind. This dish is best eaten with someone you know extremely well (or want to get to know better). For me, that's the Vicar.

200g dried linguine or spaghetti
2 large eggs
2 tablespoons thick double cream
2 tablespoons white wine
120g smoked salmon trimmings
   (much cheaper than whole slices)

juice of $\frac{1}{2}$ small lemon
salt and pepper (optional)
knob of butter (optional)

Put the pasta in a large pan of salted, boiling water and cook according to the instructions on the packet or until al dente (usually about 10 minutes). Meanwhile, beat the eggs in a bowl with a fork and stir in the cream. When the pasta is ready, drain it well, return it to the pan on the heat and pour over the wine. Let it bubble away for a couple of minutes or until the liquid has reduced a bit. Take the pan off the heat and quickly stir in the creamy egg mixture, then the smoked salmon and lemon juice. Add seasoning and the butter, if you wish. And then SLURP.

serves 2

My Hairdresser's Pasta

It's not often that you go for a haircut and come out with a recipe, as well as shorter hair. However, this is what happened when I saw Marco a few weeks ago. We got onto the subject of food and cooking and he started reminiscing about the food back home in Sardinia. So evocative was his description of his favourite pasta dish of rocket pesto and prawns that I virtually ran out of the hairdressers to buy the ingredients whilst they were still fresh in my mind.

This recipe makes 250ml of pesto, but any that's unused will keep for a week in the fridge in a sealed jar. Just make sure you cover the top of the pesto with olive oil before sealing.

For the pesto:
50g pine nuts
1 garlic clove, peeled but left whole
finely grated zest of 2 lemons
125g rocket
100ml olive oil
70g Parmesan or Grana Padano cheese (which is cheaper), finely grated

salt (optional)
200g dried, long, thin pasta of your choice, such as capellini, linguine or spaghetti
200g cooked tiger prawns, peeled (optional)

First, make the rocket pesto. Put the pine nuts into a dry frying pan and toast them lightly over a medium heat, tossing them around the pan from time to time. Tip out onto a plate, and when they are cool, put them in a food processor (using the smallest bowl, if yours has one) with the garlic, lemon zest, rocket and a third of the olive oil. Blend until it's all amalgamated, then gradually add more olive oil until the pesto is sloppy, but not runny. Stir in the cheese, have a taste and decide if you want to add any salt (I didn't, as the cheese was pretty salty).

Now cook the pasta in a large pan of boiling salted water according to the instructions on the packet or until al dente, then drain it and put it back into the hot pan. With the heat on low, stir in enough of the pesto to coat the pasta. If you are adding the prawns, wait right until the end, as they just need to be heated through very gently. Give everything a last stir, serve in hot bowls, and say 'Grazie, Marco'.

using up the pesto

You can, of course, use the leftover pesto with pasta again when it takes your fancy, or you can wash and dry a baked potato, prick it all over, then roll it first in olive oil and then salt. Place it directly on the top shelf of the oven and bake it for about 1–1½ hours (depending on its size) at 200°C/Gas Mark 6. Meanwhile, take the pesto out of the fridge and combine 1 tablespoon of it with ½ tablespoon of crème fraiche. When the potato is ready, hold it in a tea towel and push it into the middle from either side to split the skin. Pile in the creamy pesto and serve with a sweet cherry tomato and red onion salad. (This serves one, so multiply the quantities according to how many people the leftover pesto can stretch to.)

serves 2

This is a very simple treat for two people. Take a 250g vacuum-pack of halloumi and cut the cheese into slices about 5mm thick. Heat up a ridged griddle pan or frying pan until smoking hot. Cook the cheese on each side for a few minutes until beginning to look golden brown and oozy. Meanwhile, heat 1 tablespoon of the pesto in a small pan with enough olive oil to slacken it – about 2 tablespoons should do it. Divide the hot cheese between two warmed plates, drizzle with the pesto dressing and serve with a salad and some good bread.

Take a sheet of fresh, shop-bought puff pastry (Dorset make a good one), and get a ready-rolled one for even more convenience. Pop it on a lightly buttered baking tray and smear on some of the rocket pesto as though it were butter, leaving 1cm of pastry around the edges pesto-free. Scatter over some halved cherry or baby plum tomatoes, or even slices of normal-sized ones. Add chunks of hard goat's cheese (such as Chèvre), some thin slices of red onion, and then bake for 30–40 minutes at 200°C/Gas Mark 6. When the tart is cooked, cool slightly and serve scattered with Parmesan shavings and fresh basil leaves, if you have some in the house. This should serve about four people.

One-pan Chicken

I pottered into an Italian deli, lured in by the huge bowls of gleaming olives in the window, and once inside, I could have drained dry my bank account. Instead, I contented myself with just three purchases; two of which ended up in that evening's supper.

To be honest, though, you don't need to make a trip to a specialist deli to make this dish; you can pick up the sunblush tomatoes and some good black olives from the deli counter of any good supermarket. Sunblush tomatoes, like sundried tomatoes, have had their inherent tomatoey sweetness drawn out of them by spending time in the sun (it has the same effect on me, actually). However, sunblush tomatoes have been wise sunbathers and haven't stayed out there until they resemble withered prunes, unlike their sundried friends. Thus they retain a plumpness, and can be chewed, but aren't chewy – if you see what I mean. If you can't find sunblush, look out for mi-cuit tomatoes, which taste the same but have had their baking done in the oven.

I used chicken thighs because, not only are they cheaper, but they are often more flavoursome, they don't dry out (like breast meat so often can), and their meatiness stands up to the deeply intense, robust flavours of the dish. And the great thing is, the whole thing is a doddle to make.

serves 4

2 tablespoons olive oil

8 good-sized free-range chicken
  thighs

salt and pepper

2 onions, peeled and chopped

2 red peppers, sliced thinly

2 garlic cloves, peeled and crushed

600ml white wine

2 x 400g tins plum tomatoes

24 sunblush tomatoes in oil, left
  whole

16 pitted black olives

Pour the olive oil (or you could use the oil from the sunblush tomatoes) into a large frying pan and warm it up over a high heat for 30 seconds or so. Sling in the chicken, season with salt and pepper, brown it on both sides and remove to a plate. Add the onions, red peppers and garlic and fry in the residual oil for around 5 minutes until soft, then pop the chicken back in and pour in the wine. Let it bubble away vigorously for 1–2 minutes, then add the rest of the ingredients and season well. Place a lid on the pan and leave it to cook for 25 minutes, turning the heat down if the bubbling gets a bit fierce.

When it was ready I put the pan, as it was, on the table and the four of us dug in, hunks of bread at the ready for dunking. This is also very good served with green vegetables, or a nice green salad. Even the Vicar, who doesn't normally go for tomatoey stuff, pronounced it 'just right'.

Fennel-scented Chicken

I love those evenings when the Vicar goes out and I can cook slightly differently. Not that I don't like being with and cooking for the Vicar – I do – but it's nice to get the chance to get a girlfriend round, drink a glass of wine and catch up on newsy titbits over food specifically designed to please a particular friend. For Irish Helen it is usually variations around salmon and potatoes. (That thing about the Irish loving potatoes is so totally true, by the way. We once had a young Irish lad to stay. I cooked 500g of Jersey Royals. I ate three; the Vicar had five and Irish Boy slowly but surely consumed the rest. What a triumph.) Anyway, as for my other girlfriends, Bex likes fairly straightforward food, Sue likes me to throw in some version of chips, and Rache likes lots of colours and flavours. This recipe, for various reasons, is a spring supper in honour of aforementioned cooking friend, Clara.

As a child I was obsessed with those hard red sweets called aniseed balls – you'd suck them for an age, and then in the middle would be the funny little black seed. This dish has a fair bit of aniseed kick, coming from the tarragon and fennel in it. To temper this, serve it with some creamy mash and some sweet carrots tossed in butter and a squeeze of lemon.

serves 4

1 tablespoon olive oil

20g butter, plus 1 teaspoon to serve

4 chicken suprêmes (you can get
these in the butcher's; they are
breasts with an extra little bone
left on. Use good, large breasts if
you can't get those)

1 leek, cleaned and finely sliced

2 garlic cloves, peeled and crushed

1/2 fennel bulb, finely sliced

2 onions, peeled and finely chopped

175ml white wine

2 teaspoons fresh tarragon, chopped

2 tablespoons crème fraîche

salt and pepper

In a frying pan, heat the olive oil and the 20g of butter. Brown the chicken
pieces gently, remove them to a plate and then add the leek, garlic, fennel and
onions and sauté for about 5 minutes or until soft but not brown. Bung the
chicken back in the pan, pour in the wine and let it boil away until reduced
by half. Put a lid on the pan, lower the heat and gently cook its contents for
20–25 minutes or until the chicken is tender. Finally, throw in the tarragon,
the crème fraîche and the remaining teaspoon of butter. Season with salt and
pepper and serve.

If you have leftovers for another day, simply reheat them either in a
microwave or on the hob, but make sure that you bring it up to boiling point
and let it cook away for a good few minutes. Stir 1 tablespoon or so of water
into the pan during cooking if it looks a bit scarce on the sauce front.

Cheat's Salmon Fishcakes

In my butcher's display I spotted some delightful-looking salmon fishcakes. Made by a small company, they were dinky in size and shaped like fish, and I knew my children would love them. Indeed, they did, and so did I, when I selfishly raided their plates. The only thing was, these perfect little 'fishies' cost an absolute packet. I assumed that was down to the use of a vast quantity of top-notch ingredients so, intrigued, I rescued the packet from the bin and looked to see what was in them. I kid you not, these blighters contained the following: salmon, potato, tomato ketchup (yes, really) and breadcrumbs. On reflection, I remembered that the salmon fishcakes at The Ivy restaurant, in London, also contain tomato ketchup. So, if it's good enough for them …

Anyway, I went on a hunt for fish-shaped cake cutters and this is what ensued. Of course, for adults you can just use normal pastry cutters. If you really have to, that is.

These fishcakes can be made ahead and frozen; so all you need to do is defrost them for a couple of hours before cooking or take them out of the freezer in the morning and pop them in the fridge for the day.

serves 4

500g floury maincrop potatoes,
   such as King Edwards or Maris
   Piper
2 tablespoons tomato ketchup

1 teaspoon English mustard
salt and pepper
500g salmon fillets
plain flour, for dusting

First, peel the potatoes and cut them into small chunks. Pop them in a large pan of salted boiling water and cook until soft. Depending on how small you have cut up the potatoes, this should take around 20–25 minutes. When they are ready, drain them in a colander, leave to dry off slightly and for the steam to die down, and then put them in a large bowl and give them a good mash, adding the ketchup, mustard and seasoning. The potato should look comically pink now – which was just how my older sister ate it as a teenager. I used to prefer dipping forkfuls of mash into my tomato sauce, but this was not my sister; for her it was Barbie-pink potato every time.

Anyway, whilst the spuds are cooking, poach the salmon in a frying pan in enough water to cover. You want them to reach the state of absolutely only-just-cookedness; in other words, you should be able to pull off large, shiny flakes. This should take around 7 minutes at a gentle simmer. Take the salmon out of the pan with a fish slice and, when it is cool enough, skin it (if it isn't skinned already), and pull off large flakes. Reserve the fish water if you want to use it for a sauce.

Add the salmon to the potato and stir it all together to combine, taking care not to break up the fish too much. Tip the mixture out on to a lightly floured surface and pat it out until it is about 2cm thick. Take the cutters and cut out

162   Cheat's Salmon Fishcakes   serves 4

the cakes, placing each one on a flat plate or a board. Put the cakes in the fridge for 1 hour or the freezer for 30 minutes to firm up. After that, dip them lightly in flour so they are covered in a light dusting.

At this point you can either freeze some or all of them, or you can cook them straight away. Simply fry them gently on both sides, turning them only once as they are delicate little creatures. When they are nicely golden, pop them in an oven at 190°C/Gas Mark 5 for 5 minutes to ensure they are heated through.

Serve with some peas and sweetcorn and roasted baby tomatoes and a sauce of your choice: ketchup, tartare sauce or maybe a raita made from mixing finely chopped cucumber, chopped garlic and chopped fresh coriander into seasoned Greek yogurt. Even better, you could make a quick sauce by frying a finely chopped shallot in a knob of butter until soft, throwing in 120ml of wine and 120ml of the water used to cook the fish, bringing it to the boil and allowing the liquid to reduce by at least half. Then pour in some cream – a 287ml carton should do it. Allow the sauce to thicken somewhat until it coats the back of a spoon, then add 1 tablespoon of chopped herbs: chives, tarragon or sorrel, if you can find any. Add the juice of ½ lemon and season well. This sauce can also be used to liven up fish in general or even, if you leave out the fishy water and swap it with more wine, a plain breast of chicken.

Creamy Smoked Haddock Puff Pastry Pie

Don't you just love the words 'puff pastry pie'? I can't say them without adopting a North Yorkshire accent and secretly imagining I have started running a cosy pub on the Moors that offers up pies, fires and ales to passing wayfarers. Back in a less romantic reality, I cooked this pie on a freezing evening in London for a gang of the Vicar's work colleagues. As he has recently changed his role and has departed parish life to run a big conference, his meeting was with the likes of sound engineers and technical types. There was one non-meat eater attending, so I opted for fish, but as the evening was dark, bleak and freezing I wanted to serve something homely and hearty. A pie was the answer. With its pastry top, this fish pie is a bit less hassle than the usual potato-topped ones. And that's always a good thing on a weekday.

7 eggs, at room temperature
1kg undyed smoked haddock
200ml white wine
300ml water
185g spinach, washed well
60g butter
1 red onion, peeled and finely
    chopped
50g plain flour

300ml double cream
30g chives (about 6 tablespoons)
3 handfuls of Cheddar cheese
juice of 1 lemon
pepper
375g bought, chilled puff pastry,
    ready-rolled

You will need a 2-litre dish. Mine was oblong, measuring 28cm x 19cm.

Boil the kettle and pour the water into a large pan. Slip 6 of the eggs gently into the water and bring back to the boil. Leave them in the pan for 7 minutes, then pour away the water and cool the eggs under the cold tap.

Meanwhile, put the fish in another large pan with the wine and the water. Bring the liquid to the boil, then turn the heat down and let the haddock poach for 3 minutes. Then scoop out the haddock using a fish slice and leave it to cool. Reserve the poaching liquid. Now put the spinach in another pan on its own – the residual water from the washing is all it needs – cover with a lid and allow the spinach to cook until just wilted. This should only take 1–2 minutes. When it's done, tip it into a colander to cool. When it has done so, squeeze out any water with your hands and chop the spinach up roughly – I find using kitchen scissors is the easiest way to do this.

Now decant the reserved fish poaching liquid into a jug and add the butter to the pan it has vacated. Once it has melted, add the chopped onion and fry until softened. Stir in the flour and let it cook for a couple of minutes before gradually adding the liquid from the jug, stirring enthusiastically all the while. Once it's all in, leave to simmer for a few minutes until it has thickened nicely. Add the cream and the chives and let it bubble away for a few minutes until the sauce is unctuously glossy. Take the pan off the heat, grate the cheese and throw it in the pan along with the lemon juice and lots of pepper. (I didn't add salt as the smoked haddock tastes quite salty enough.)

Next, quickly skin the fish, break it into large chunks and put it in the baking dish. Peel the eggs, quarter them and add them to the dish, scattering them evenly around the flakes of haddock so that everyone gets a chance to have some. Lay the spinach over the top, again spreading it around to give everyone a fair share. Now pour over the sauce and carefully lay the pastry over the top. At this point I was chuffed I'd gone for an oblong dish, as the pastry was a perfect fit and I only had to trim a bit off, using the trimmings to make a little design for the top of the pie. Beat the remaining egg, crimp the edges of the pastry, brush with the beaten egg and poke a few holes in the top of the pie with a fork or a sharp knife. Cook in the oven for around 30–40 minutes at 190°C/Gas Mark 5 until the pie filling is hot and the pastry crisp and golden. Serve with little boiled new potatoes and some steamed broccoli.

A Proper Midweek Stew

We'd had a big leg of lamb on the Sunday and I'd made some stock with the bones. Time to make a proper, old-fashioned stew. Comforting and gentle, not too tasking, there are times when a stew hits all the right notes. Sure, winter is the time to bury your face in creamy mash and sticky puds, but a stew, proudly plain, can be just what you are after, after a long, hard day, especially if you are feeling tired and a bit under the weather. It's like going home to someone kind and undemanding, who exists merely to stroke your hair and soothe your soul.

Make this at the weekend or whenever you have time (it can be frozen). If you can stop yourself slipping it down then and there once you've cooked it, it will even taste better the next day. You could also put potato in this, but I'm not fond of its consistency after being cooked for a long time. Or, for extra ballast, you could add some soaked dried or tinned beans – flageolet or cannellini are good. I just served my simple version with lots of good bread.

around 560g lamb neck fillet

3 tablespoons olive oil

2 onions, peeled and thickly sliced

4 carrots, peeled and chopped into
2cm lengths

2 leeks, cleaned and chopped into
2cm lengths

1 swede, peeled and chopped into
2cm chunks

3 garlic cloves, peeled and crushed

1 large tablespoon plain flour

750ml lamb stock (fresh, or use a
good-quality liquid bouillon)

8 small sprigs of thyme, leaves
removed (or just throw in the
sprigs whole – the leaves will
come off during cooking)

salt and pepper

Cut up the lamb into 2cm chunks and heat the oil in a large flameproof casserole dish – I used my medium-sized cauldron. Once the oil is hot, add the lamb and cook it until nicely browned; you'll need to give it a stir now and again. Now add the vegetables and garlic and stir. Let it cook gently for around 5 minutes, then stir in the flour. Stir for a few minutes, then gradually add the stock. Bring the stew to the boil, turn the heat down to low, stir in the thyme leaves or sprigs and let it bubble gently away for 1½–2 hours. Noting the stew's beautiful colours, remove the thyme stalks, if necessary, add salt and pepper to taste and either serve or allow it to cool, cover and pop it in the fridge. The next day, look forward to slurping out of a big bowl once you've gently reheated it on top of the stove, stirring now and then, until piping hot.

A Richer Lamb Stew

This is also lamb swimming in liquid, but it isn't the plain sort of stew that Granny used to make: it is far more luxurious and, with the wine, more expensive. It is delicious served with some sort of mash. When I made it the Vicar was delighted that there was a bowl of leftovers, which he took to work the next day in a little Tupperware box. He even offered tastes of it to the girls in the office, generous man that he is.

2 tablespoons olive oil
500g cubed lamb, shoulder or neck
    fillets (using neck brings the cost
    down)
4 carrots, peeled and cut across into
    thick chunks
5 onions, peeled and thickly sliced
10 Jerusalem artichokes, peeled and
    sliced into 5mm slices

2 garlic cloves, peeled and crushed
1 x 75cl bottle red wine
10 sprigs of thyme
2 x 400g tins chopped tomatoes
salt and pepper
2 teaspoons runny honey

Heat the oil in a large, flameproof casserole or pan and brown the meat in batches, if necessary. I chose not to flour the meat because, after reducing the sauce, it wasn't in the least watery. When it's nicely rusty-coloured, remove to a plate and throw in the fresh vegetables and garlic. (Feel free to substitute the Jerusalem artichokes with something like celeriac or swede, if you prefer. I love Jerusalem artichokes, but I have to say that they are a pig to peel, with all their bumps and nodules.) Soften the vegetables in the oil and then return the lamb back to the pan, sloshing in the red wine straight after, along with the thyme. Bring the wine to the boil, then add the tomatoes and lots of black pepper.

serves 4

When it's all bubbling away merrily, turn the heat down to low and cover the pot with a lid. Cook gently for about 2½ hours or until the liquid has reduced and the lamb is tender. Add salt, and a touch of sweetness in the form of the honey. Again, this is even better if made in advance and reheated gently on the top of the stove until piping hot.

see page 112

Leeky Mash

White Chocolate and Amaretto Ice Cream see page 130

see page 136

Pear Chocolate Betty

Fennel-scented Chicken

see page 159

see page 164

Creamy Smoked Haddock Puff Pastry Pie

Quick and Easy Fish Stew

see page 171

see page 171

Quick and Easy Fish Stew

Sage for Herby Pork Chops see page 182

A Quick and Easy Fish Stew

Yet another stew, but this time with fish. I would use a cheap white fish for this, such as pollack or coley. It has to be said that coley looks as grey as old pants before it's cooked, but once it's hot it's as white and shiny as cod. This stew is a poor man's version of my halibut on clam stew on page 100. The ingredients do vary a little, and here the fish goes in the pot at the end in chunks, rather than being fried separately. The result is certainly not as refined, but it is tasty nonetheless; the flavour infused with both warmth from the chilli and freshness from the herbs and lemon. We ate it with friends, bowls on our laps and good bread at the ready for dunking.

500g cheap white fish

1kg mussels

1¹/₂ tablespoons olive oil

4 shallots, peeled and finely
    chopped

2 celery sticks, finely chopped

2 garlic cloves, peeled and crushed

125ml white wine

2 x 400g tins chopped tomatoes

¹/₂ teaspoon red chilli (or use 'Lazy
    Chilli' from a jar), de-seeded and
    finely chopped

1 tablespoon parsley, chopped

2 handfuls of basil, torn up finely

juice of 1 lemon

salt and pepper

Cut the fish into large chunks and set aside. Put the mussels in a big bowl of cold water and pull out any beards, discarding any mussels that are not clamped shut after their dip in the water.

Heat the oil in a large flameproof pan (as ever, I used one of my cauldrons) and gently fry the shallots, celery and garlic for about 4–5 minutes until softened. Pour in the wine and the tomatoes and bring to the boil. Once it's bubbling away, turn down the heat a touch and let it simmer away for 10–15 minutes. Add the mussels, cover with a lid and cook for about 5 minutes or until the mussels have opened. Add the chunks of white fish a couple of minutes after the mussels have gone in. They won't take any time to cook and may still disintegrate – mine did. This is a shame in some ways, but it doesn't impair the taste, and any fishy mushiness will just add to the texture of the broth. Add the chilli, adding extra if you want more of a kick, then throw in the herbs and lemon juice, retaining a little of the basil. Taste for seasoning and add salt and pepper to taste. Ladle out into warmed bowls, sprinkle over the rest of the basil and serve as fast as you can.

a different sort of fish stew

If mussels aren't your thing and you want to use the cheap white fish but make the stew taste fishier, just fry the vegetables and then, when you add the tomatoes and wine, throw in 2 or 3 finely chopped anchovy fillets. These will dissolve in the stew, so even if people say they don't like anchovies they will never be able to tell they are there. Double the amount of white fish suggested in the ingredients list and cook it through, adding a handful of rinsed and drained capers instead of the chilli, and adding the lemon juice and herbs at the end, as above.

Storecupboard Stew

Don't look down on me for the studenty suggestion that I'm about to make. I offer it, with humility, for those nights when you have virtually nothing in the house and your hand is hovering over the phone to dial the take-away down the road that brings food that makes you feel rotten and costs far more than it should. I suggest, nay, shout: save your money for better things and use the stuff in your kitchen. I confess, I know this isn't really recipe-book fare – it is merely a strident message to you to open those cupboard doors, however sparse, and have a rummage. So easily we overlook the simple, but possible, in favour of salty, fatty junk. I know there are times when that is the only thing we want – no – need. I once observed that my friend, the venerable Doctor S, who loves good food and is an excellent cook, was eating rather too many tinned pies. 'What!' I said. 'You have five of them? Stacked up and ready for use?! Just what is going on?' However, all too soon, on a rainy day of misery, I was forced to send the Doctor a meek and somewhat embarrassed text:

Elisa: 'I just ate one.'

Doctor S: 'And …?'

Elisa: 'Bother, I quite liked it.'

This recipe is better for you than a tinned pie and will take less time than that said pie to cook. Then go to bed, dreaming of what you buy with the money you could have thrown at a take-away – or that awful pie.

1 tablespoon olive oil
1 onion, peeled and chopped
1 garlic clove, peeled and crushed
1 x 400g tin tomatoes
1 teaspoon dried oregano, or mixed
   herbs, or herbes de Provence

1 x 410g tin chickpeas (or any sort of
   beans except the baked ones!)
1 x 200g tin tuna
$^{1}/_{4}$ teaspoon harissa paste (or use
   'Lazy Chilli' from a jar)
salt and pepper

In a large flameproof pan or casserole, heat the oil and fry the onion and garlic until golden. Add the tomatoes and the dried herbs, or whichever of the flavourings you are going for, and cook for a couple of minutes before throwing in the chickpeas. Once it's all bubbling, stir in the tuna and add the harissa or chilli at the end. Taste, season, and serve with rice, a baked potato, or whatever you have to hand.

Posh Spice Curry

We live in a celebrity-obsessed culture that sees many of us gobble up the gossip mags for titbits on who is wearing what, doing what and even eating what. Apparently Posh Spice, aka Mrs David Beckham, and one of the most photographed women today, is currently eating edamame beans by the barrel full. I can't honestly imagine her eating anything in carefree abandon, so let's just say she is partial to one or two.

It's a sensible choice. These beans, the baby version of soya beans, are packed full of protein and all-round goodness. I have to say that for the normal cook, tracking down these healthy little numbers isn't always easy. I'd try a Japanese supermarket, or you may be able to buy them online, and some supermarkets sell them frozen already podded, which is what you need here. If you really can't track them down in any form, you can use soya beans here instead; Bird's Eye do them and you'll find them in the freezer aisle.

If you can find edamame beans fresh in their pods, boil them for a few minutes and eat them as a snack, popping each bean out of its pod before dropping them into your mouth. Dip them in a bit of salt, if you wish. Japanese restaurants often serve them as an appetiser; a lovely thing to nibble on whilst menu choices are made or whilst waiting for the main dish to come.

serves 4

Japanese curry is very popular, chiefly because it is so easy to cook. The Japanese have a whole range of sticky curry sauce blocks, which they use to create the sauce. I have to say, I instinctively baulk at using ready-made sauces, and did so when I read the ingredients on the packet. However, using these rather unreal commercial cooking aides is all right once in a blue moon, and the result was sweet, thick and altogether rather different from an Indian curry. And anyway, I had to make it to gratify my silly, childish mind: by combining these precious beans, beloved by Mrs Beckham, with a rather overly manufactured curry sauce, I got Posh Spice (an unlikely candidate to be mentioned in a recipe book) on a plate.

1½ tablespoons groundnut oil
2 large onions, peeled and sliced
2 garlic cloves, peeled and crushed
1 large carrot, peeled and sliced into 5mm pieces
1 yellow or orange pepper, cored and chopped into bite-sized pieces
10 button mushrooms, wiped clean and halved

600ml cold water
1 packet medium-hot Japanese curry mix, such as 'Golden Curry'
200g shelled edamame beans, fresh or frozen and out of their pods
sticky Japanese rice or noodles, to serve

Heat the oil in a large pan, add the onions and garlic and soften them for 1–2 minutes. Meanwhile, cut each slice of carrot into quarters. Add the carrot to the pan and cook over a medium heat, stirring occasionally, for 3 minutes or so. Now add the pepper, cook for another minute and then throw in the mushrooms. Add the water, bring to the boil and slam on a lid. With the heat at medium, let the vegetables simmer away for around 10 minutes or so, or until softened. If you are using frozen soya beans, which are older than their edamame siblings, you may want to cook them separately at this point – for 3 minutes or so in boiling salted water – then drain them under cold running water and slip off their skins.

After a while this job, initially irritating, is actually quite enjoyable; in a mind-numbing sort of way. Think of it like opening lots of wrapped sweets. Once the vegetables are soft, add the sticky curry mix (you'll need the whole pack) and stir it in. Replace the lid and cook for another 5 minutes, adding the beans in the last minute or so to warm through. If you have tracked down edamame beans they can be added, uncooked, in the last 3–4 minutes of the cooking time. Check they are cooked, then serve the curry.

Traditionally, Japanese curry is served with sticky Japanese rice or noodles; the rice served on the left of the plate, the curry on the right, with some sauce poured over the rice in the middle.

serves 4

Debbie's Thai Curry

I'm not a girl who craves an Indian and a can of beer on a Friday night. However, a Thai curry is another matter. Its fresh, almost biting, fragrance lifts my spirits. I think this dish is the perfect way to start a lazy weekend and this version, provided by Debbie, is fabulous.

For the curry paste:

3 stalks lemongrass

1 teaspoon cumin seeds

1 teaspoon coriander seeds

5 red chillies (fresh, or use 'Lazy Chilli' from a jar), de-seeded and finely chopped

3cm piece fresh root ginger, peeled and finely grated

6 garlic cloves, peeled and chopped

3 shallots, peeled and chopped

¼ teaspoon *blachan* (this is Thai shrimp paste; it really stinks, so keep it in the fridge in a VERY airtight container)

2 teaspoons paprika

½ teaspoon turmeric

1 teaspoon salt

1 tablespoon sunflower oil

For the liquidy bit:

2 tablespoons sunflower oil

1 x 400ml tin coconut milk

150ml chicken stock (fresh, or use a good-quality liquid bouillon)

2 teaspoons light soft brown sugar (or palm sugar)

juice of 1 lime, plus extra to taste (optional)

2–4 fresh kaffir lime leaves (optional)

2 tablespoons Thai fish sauce, plus extra to taste (optional)

outer leaves from the lemongrass

350g raw tiger prawns, peeled, or 350g mixed seafood and fish, or 350g raw chicken breast or beef (cut into strips), or 1 butternut, crown prince or kabocha squash, peeled and sliced

150g bamboo shoots, sugar snaps or mangetouts, sliced

2 tablespoons fresh basil leaves (or Thai holy basil, if you can get it)

First, make the curry paste. Take the stalks of lemongrass and remove the top third of each stalk. Then pull away a few layers of the outer coarser leaves (setting these aside to use later), and finely chop the tender core. Grind the cumin and coriander seeds in a blender, or pound them in a pestle and mortar. Pop these and all the other paste ingredients into a food processor and whizz to combine, scraping the mixture down from the sides every now and then, if necessary, until you have a smooth paste.

Heat the oil in a large pan or a wok and add the curry paste. Fry over a medium heat for 2–3 minutes, stirring, until the smell in the kitchen is fragrantly aromatic and the paste has begun to split away from the oil. Add the coconut milk, stock, sugar, the lime juice, kaffir lime leaves and Thai fish sauce if using, and the reserved outer leaves of the lemongrass, and bring to the boil, stirring once or twice. Simmer gently for 2–3 minutes more. Add the prawns, fish, meat or vegetables (depending on what you are using), with the bamboo shoots or green vegetables, and cook briefly – a couple of minutes should do it. Remove the lemongrass leaves and stir in the basil leaves.

Serve with plain Thai jasmine rice in deep, warmed soup bowls. Don't panic if the curry isn't thick and glutinous: flavour-packed it will be, heavily rich it won't.

Thai Jasmine Rice

Sticky and clumpy, this bland, calming rice is the ideal accompaniment to Debbie's sparky Thai curry.

350g Thai jasmine rice
600ml boiling water

Put the rice into a sieve and rinse it under cold water until the water runs from milky white to almost clear. Drain it well and tip into a medium-sized pan. Pour over the boiling water and bring to the boil, stirring once. Cover and reduce the heat to low. Cook for 15 minutes and then leave on the side, lid on, for 5 minutes before serving.

My Sausage and Mash

A trip round a food market with the family and my cousin was topped off with steaming plates of sausage and mash in a bustling café. Driving back, the cousin reminded me of my own version that I once made for her. She loved it so much that she had memorised the method and made it endlessly until her husband begged for mercy. Now, however, he is in an obsessive broth-making period and giving the lovely girl a taste of her own medicine.

The secret of this recipe is in the rosé wine. Lighter than red, it gives the gravy/sauce a fruity lightness that combines perfectly with the sweet richness of the plum tomatoes. This isn't your usual bangers and rich-onion gravy, but something rather more fragrant.

1 tablespoon olive oil
8–12 good-quality sausages
1 onion, peeled and finely chopped
1 garlic clove, peeled and crushed
100g baby plum tomatoes, halved

250ml rosé wine
175ml double cream
salt and pepper
wholegrain and Dijon mustard, to serve

In a large frying pan, heat the oil and lightly brown the sausages all over on a lowish heat. When they are around halfway to being cooked, add the onion and garlic and cook until soft and golden. Throw in the tomatoes and crush into the pan a little before pouring in the wine and cream. Allow the sauce to thicken and reduce, then season well before serving with the mash on page 18 or 112. Make sure there's some mustard around for those who want it.

Herby Pork Chops with Roasted New Potatoes

Chops take me right back to my childhood and remind me of my mother sacrificing the meat to gain crisply brown fat: our secret guilty pleasure. I wouldn't suggest you do that here, though. Instead, buy some healthy-looking organic chops and cook them carefully, as there is nothing worse than dried-out pork. If you are eating with young children you may want to leave out the herbs and the sage and lemon cream, but I guarantee they will love the dinky little potatoes.

For the roasted new potatoes:
500g baby new potatoes
1 garlic clove, peeled and crushed
3 tablespoons olive oil
salt and pepper

For the herby pork chops:
1 dessertspoon dried myrtle leaves
3 garlic cloves, peeled and 2 crushed
    separately

6 sprigs of thyme, leaves removed
4 organic pork chops (about 175g
    each)

For the sage and lemon cream:
200ml double cream
8 sage leaves
juice of 1 lemon
salt and pepper

The potatoes take the longest to cook, so prepare these before you start on the pork. Preheat the oven to 220°C/Gas Mark 7. Wash the potatoes and cut any that are a bit big into two. Mix the garlic with the oil and pour it into a roasting tin. Throw in the potatoes, season them generously, and put them in the oven. Turn the oven down to 200°C/Gas Mark 6 after 20 minutes, when the pork makes its entrance.

In a pestle and mortar, bang together the myrtle leaves with 2 of the garlic cloves and all the thyme leaves. Anoint the chops with the paste on one side only and place them in a roasting tin. Cook in the oven at 200°C/Gas Mark 6 for about 20 minutes or until cooked through.

To make the sage and lemon cream pour the double cream into a bowl and, using kitchen scissors, snip the sage leaves into fine strips. Pop the leaves in a mortar and pound the leaves with the pestle to release their full aroma. Add the sage and lemon juice to the cream and combine, then season with lots of salt and pepper.

Pour it into a small pan and warm it through just before serving – it should only take about 5 minutes. Serve alongside the roasted new potatoes and herby pork chops.

Cod with Smoky-sweet Salsa and Warm Puy Lentil Salad

It is so easy to forget about those bags of dried stuff, like lentils and quinoa, sitting around in the cupboard. You bring them home from the supermarket, excited and feeling oh-so-worthy at their healthiness – and promptly forget about them. I have to say that I am particularly bad at this, as the Vicar wouldn't naturally go for this sort of thing. However, when I tell him how cheap it is, even he happily slips it down.

If you prefer, you could use another thick white fish instead of the cod, such as pollack for this dish. White fish can taste quite plain to some palates, so here I've beefed things up a bit with a full-flavoured warm salsa of smoky pancetta, sweet red onions and cherry tomatoes. The balsamic vinegar thrown in at the end adds fruitiness, and with the earthiness of the warm lentils this combination comes together to make a pleasing plate of rather good food. If you have any salsa left over, the salsa would make a great pasta sauce, or would be rather tasty with a baked potato. It would also be equally at home served with a piece of chicken.

When I first made this dish I'd forgotten to buy some fresh parsley. However, the Vicar kindly picked some up for me. As he was taking it to the till he heard a woman exclaim loudly: 'Oh, my! Look, there's a cockroach! I don't do cockroaches.' At which point she fled the shop. My brave man persevered with his purchase, and thankfully no foreign crunchiness was perceived in the finished dish.

4 slices of cod or pollack (about 175g each)
salt and pepper
1 tablespoon olive oil

For the warm Puy lentil salad:
200g Puy lentils
200ml white wine
200ml water
2 tablespoons olive oil
1 medium onion, peeled and finely chopped
juice of 1 lemon

1 tablespoon fresh parsley, chopped
salt and pepper

For the salsa:
2 tablespoons olive oil
2 medium red onions, peeled and finely chopped
2 garlic cloves, peeled and crushed
300g pancetta
16 cherry tomatoes, diced into quarters
2 tablespoons balsamic vinegar
salt and pepper

First make the Puy lentil salad. Rinse the lentils under running water and then drain. Put them in a pan with the wine and water (or just use all water, if you prefer). Don't add salt at this stage, or it will make the lentils go tough. Bring it all to the boil and then simmer for 15–20 minutes or until the lentils are cooked but still firm.

While the lentils are cooking, heat the oil in a pan. Add the chopped onions and cook until soft and translucent. Take them off the heat and stir in the lemon juice. When the lentils are ready, stir in the onion mixture along with the chopped parsley and lots of salt and pepper.

To make the salsa, heat the oil in a frying pan, add the onions and the garlic and soften gently. Now throw in the pancetta and cook until it is beginning to crisp up. Finally, add the tomatoes and mush them gently into the pan using the back of a wooden spoon. When the tomatoes have lost their shape and released their sweet juices, pour in the balsamic vinegar and cook to allow some of the vinegary essence to evaporate. Season with some salt and pepper, to taste, then remove from the heat while you prepare the fish.

Preheat the oven to 200°C/Gas Mark 6. Season the fish with lots of salt and pepper. Heat the oil in a frying pan and put in the cod, skin-side down. Cook until the skin is golden and crispy, then immediately transfer the cod, skin-side up, to an ovenproof dish. Pile the salsa on top of, and around, the cod. When you are ready to cook it, pop the dish into the oven for 7–10 minutes or until the cod is tender. Serve with the warm Puy lentil salad.

Superfood Supper

Superfoods. What a silly word. To my mind, any food, in moderation, has its own power and healthy-giving or happy-making properties. For me, chocolate cake, black pudding and pork scratchings all have their right place. However, this dish revels in its on-trend foray into the world of the so-called superfood. Look at your plate and those smug little antioxidants could almost rise up and slap you in the face. Pomegranates, goji berries, nuts and wheat all conspire to make a meal that should make you feel incredibly virtuous. The good news is, eating it won't make you feel you have joined a health farm. Nutritious it may be. But it will make you happy too.

200g bulgar wheat	2 tablespoons olive oil
6 spring onions, finely chopped	1 leek (just the white part), cleaned
50g unsalted pistachio nuts	160g sugar snaps
1 tablespoon sundried goji berries	1 pomegranate
1 tablespoon raisins	300g feta cheese, cut into cubes
7 ready-to-eat dried apricots, chopped small	1 tablespoon fresh parsley, chopped
	salt and pepper

Put the bulgar wheat in a pan with 2 pints of water and place on a high heat. Bring everything to the boil, then simmer for 10–15 minutes. In a large bowl, mix the spring onions, pistachio nuts and all the dried fruit. Heat the olive oil in a pan and meanwhile cut the leek horizontally and slice it finely. Add it to the pan and cook until softened. Add the sugar snaps for the last 2–3 minutes of the cooking time.

serves 4–6

By the end of the cooking time the bulgar wheat should have absorbed all the water. When the vegetables are cooked, add them, with their oil, to the bulgar wheat and tip all this into the bowl of fruit and nuts. Next, cut the pomegranate in half and bang out the seeds into the bowl, squeezing out any juice at the same time. Throw in the cubed feta and stir in gently, along with the parsley and seasoning and a bit more olive oil, if you wish and serve.

My Tortilla

I used to hate eggs; then, one day, in my pre-carnivore times, I sat myself down one morning with a softly boiled number. After all, I needed the protein. 'What are you doing?' said the Vicar, as he joined me at the table. 'Have you lost your mind?'

I managed to slip it down, and the next day I stomached a poached one; the day after, it was scrambled and, finally, it was fried. After my egg assault course I am now egg-crazy. I am not sure what the verdict is on cholesterol these days, but I'd happily eat eggs every day of the week.

A Vicar-favourite, this tortilla easily serves four at supper. Serve it with a salad, maybe some garlic mayonnaise, and, if you want to throw in any extras, chorizo, spring onions, ham – that's up to you. I confess, however, that I am of the plain and perfect tortilla school. If you have any left over, eat it cold for lunch the next day.

300ml olive oil
5 large, old potatoes, peeled and thinly sliced (I used my mandolin)
1 medium onion, peeled and finely chopped

2 garlic cloves, peeled and crushed
6 large eggs
salt and pepper

serves 4

Heat the oil in a large frying pan over a medium heat and add the potato slices. Move them around to cook in the oil and then, after 5 minutes of cooking, add the onion and garlic. Stir it about a bit, then put on a lid and cook until the potatoes are soft and yielding. At this point, take them out of the pan and drain them in a colander, retaining around 3 tablespoons of the oil in the pan.

Whisk the eggs in a large bowl with a big pinch of salt and tip in the oniony potato mix. You could now leave it mulling for a bit, as it seems to benefit from that. Pour the mixture into a large frying pan and cook on a medium heat until half-set. Heat the grill and put the frying pan under it to cook the top of the tortilla.

I like my tortilla at room temperature, or even cold, but if you are hungry and have to eat immediately, I promise not to shout abuse.

Rancheros Eggs

I know this recipe is in no way authentic, but this eggy combo is enough to send me on a boat to the sun. I remember sitting on a rather lovely terrace, having just got off a plane, eating something rather similar. (It was in my foolish vegetarian days.) Cooking this reminds me of that huskily warm night, and the fact that the simple things – like beans on toast after a Saturday swim, or a perfectly ripe peach in the summer – can often give us more pleasure than far fancier fare.

2 tablespoons olive oil
1 large onion, peeled and chopped
1 large red pepper, core removed
    and cut into thin strips
2 garlic cloves, peeled and crushed
2 green chillies, de-seeded and
    finely chopped
1 teaspoon ground cumin
600g tinned chopped tomatoes

1 teaspoon lime juice
salt and pepper
4 large eggs
2 tablespoons fresh coriander,
    chopped
warm flour tortillas, for scooping
    and dipping

Heat the oil in a large, deep frying pan. Add the onion and pepper and fry gently for about 5 minutes until both are soft and the onion very lightly browned. Add the garlic, chillies and ground cumin and fry for another minute. Add the tomatoes and simmer gently, stirring now and then, for 10–15 minutes until reduced and slightly thickened. Stir in the lime juice and some seasoning to taste. Now make 4 deep dips in the mixture with the back of a wooden spoon and imagine them as baby birds' nests.

serves 2

Carefully break one egg into each and cover the pan with a well-fitting lid. Leave to set until cooked the way you like your eggs – about 10–12 minutes for just done. Scatter over the fresh coriander and serve with lots of those lovely warm tortillas.

Berger Lamb

Mince is the stalwart of the midweek supper. Reliable, yet infinitely flexible, it is the cheap and tasty solution when your aim is to get a hot meal on the table at the end of a busy day. Okay, *berger* is French for 'shepherd', so here I am merely offering up my version of shepherd's pie. It is a delicious one, though.

1 tablespoon olive oil
25g butter
8 rashers of rindless smoked streaky
    bacon or pancetta, finely
    chopped (about 100g)
2 medium onions, peeled and
    chopped
1 large celery stick, finely chopped
1 large carrot, peeled and finely
    chopped
2 garlic cloves, peeled and chopped
700g minced lamb
150ml red wine
200ml lamb stock (fresh, or use a
    good-quality liquid bouillon)
2 tablespoons tomato purée
2–3 fresh bay leaves
1 tablespoon fresh thyme leaves
4 tablespoons flatleaf parsley,
    chopped

salt and pepper

For the mashed potato:
1kg maincrop potatoes, such as
    King Edwards or Maris Piper
4 tablespoons hot full-fat milk
40g butter
5 spring onions, chopped, or 1 large
    tablespoon chives, chopped
freshly grated nutmeg
salt and pepper

For the crunchy cheese topping:
40g butter, melted
50g fresh white breadcrumbs
50g Gruyère or Cheddar cheese,
    coarsely grated

Heat the oil and butter in a large pan, add the bacon or pancetta and fry over a medium heat until lightly golden. Toss in the onions, celery, carrot and garlic and fry until the onions are soft, tender and gleaming. Add the minced lamb and fry, stirring until all of it is browned. Then add the wine, stock, tomato purée, herbs and seasoning. When it becomes rich, but not soupy, turn off the heat, as it will lose a little more moisture when it is in the oven.

Next, peel the potatoes and cut them into large chunks. Cook them in a pan of boiling salted water for 20 minutes until tender, drain into a colander and leave them for a few minutes to dry off slightly and for the steam to die down. Heat the milk and butter in the pan, remove it from the heat then tip in the potatoes and mash them well. Stir in the spring onions or chives, the nutmeg, and salt and pepper to taste.

Preheat the oven to 180°C/Gas Mark 4. Pile the mince into a shallow ovenproof dish and spread the mash over the top. In a small bowl, mix together the melted butter and breadcrumbs for the topping, then stir in the grated cheese. Sprinkle this over the top, then pop the dish in the oven for 30 minutes or so – it should look golden and bubbling. Serve with ketchup and frozen peas – the children will love you for it.

Italian Polpette

Polpette are the Italian version of meatballs. How does this nation always manage to make things sound so stylish, and why do we Brits insist on converting things to the pedestrian? I mean, put the words *polpette* and meatballs in the same sentence and they don't really compare; '*polpette*' sounds romantic and glamorous, while 'meatballs' evokes a wet weekend in a guesthouse with polyester sheets on the bed. But the fact is, whether you refer to them using a name that is tastefully flamboyant or one that is depressingly down-to-earth, these bite-sized treats are delicious little creatures. The Vicar, it has to be said, is enormously partial to them. He sometimes forces us all into a trip to Ikea just to partake of the Swedish version they serve up in the restaurant.

Whilst I may mock this behaviour, he does have a point. Peasant-fare meatballs may be as far away from an evening with Donatella Versace as you would ever really get, but they do taste really, really good. And come a cold Tuesday in February, you will thank me for this recipe. Obviously, if I'd bought you tickets to *The Marriage of Figaro*, or maybe even a flight to Venice, you might be even more grateful, but I hope these tasty little monsters, however ordinary, will suffice.

serves 4

For the meatballs:

3 tablespoons olive oil

1 medium onion, peeled and finely
    chopped

3 garlic cloves, peeled and crushed

120g pancetta, finely chopped

750g minced beef

finely grated zest of $\frac{1}{2}$ lemon

200g Gruyère cheese, finely grated
    (or 100g grated Parmesan cheese)

50g fresh white breadcrumbs

1–2 tablespoons fresh sage, chopped

4 tablespoons flatleaf parsley,
    chopped

$\frac{1}{2}$ teaspoon freshly grated nutmeg

1 medium egg, beaten

salt and pepper

For the tomato sauce:

1 tablespoon olive oil

20g butter

1 medium onion, peeled and finely
    chopped

1 garlic clove, peeled and crushed

1 large red pepper, core removed
    and finely chopped

1 x 200g tin chopped tomatoes

350g tomato passata

salt and pepper

2 tablespoons basil leaves, shredded

fresh or dried tagliatelle, to serve

First, make the meatballs. Heat 1 tablespoon of the olive oil in a small frying pan and cook the onion and garlic over a medium heat for 5–6 minutes until soft. Leave to cool slightly, before tipping the mixture into a large bowl with the pancetta, beef, lemon zest, Gruyère, breadcrumbs, sage, parsley and nutmeg. Mix it all together well with your hands – an experience I hope will remind you of making mud pies as a child. Add the egg, $\frac{1}{2}$ teaspoon of salt and plenty of black pepper, then shape the mixture into walnut-sized balls using slightly wet hands. Heat the remaining 2 tablespoons of oil in a large frying pan, add the meatballs, a few at a time, and brown them all over. Then transfer them to a flameproof casserole dish or large pan.

serves 4

Next, make the sauce. Heat the oil in the same large frying pan (no need to wash it) and, when it is hot, add the butter, onion, garlic and red pepper. Fry gently until softened and then add the chopped tomatoes, passata, $\frac{1}{2}$ teaspoon of salt and some black pepper. Bring it all to the boil before chucking it all over the meatballs. Cover the dish or pan with a lid and let it simmer gently on the top of the stove for 20 minutes, stirring gently now and then but taking care not to break up the meatballs. When cooked, stir in the shredded basil and serve with a big mound of fresh tagliatelle.

serves 4

Cumin-spiced Lamb Chops with Butter Bean Mash

As I've already mentioned, lamb is the Vicar's favourite meat. Childishly, I find it quite funny when he says, 'I love lamb', as Baby Lamb is the pet name my mother gave me as a child (oh dear, why did I just tell you that?!). Anyway, lamb lends itself well to fast cooking: chops, neck fillet, cubed or shredded leg all do the business in terms of speed of cooking and utter deliciousness.

The butter bean mash that accompanies the lamb is earthy stuff. The Vicar wanted more cream in it, but he loves the stuff with a passion (and never puts on any weight, the monkey).

4 teaspoons cumin seeds
2 garlic cloves, peeled and crushed
rock salt and pepper
juice of 1 lemon
2 tablespoons olive oil
4 lamb chops

For the butter bean mash:
2 x 200g tins butter beans
2 tablespoons olive oil
2 garlic cloves, peeled and crushed
juice of ¹/₂ lemon
1 tablespoon parsley, chopped
1 large tablespoon double cream
salt and pepper

First, prepare the lamb chops. In a pestle and mortar, grind together the cumin, garlic and rock salt and pepper. Swirl in the lemon and oil and anoint the chops with this headily scented mixture. Heat up a ridged griddle pan, if you have one, or a large frying pan and, once it is smoking, slap on the chops. They should take 3–4 minutes each side, depending on their thickness and how you like your meat cooked.

serves 4

Meanwhile, make the butter bean mash. Empty the beans into a colander and rinse them under the cold tap. Heat the oil in a pan and add the garlic – don't let it brown, just soften. Tip in the beans and stir them round in the oil, mashing them with a fork or a potato masher. Pour in the lemon juice, add the parsley, cream and seasoning, mashing away all the time. Once it is soft but still has texture, serve with the lovely lamb.

Lamb Kebabs with Greek Salad and Tzatziki

Neck fillets are pleasingly inexpensive and, like the perfect party guest, they are also obligingly accommodating. Happy to spend hours bubbling away on the stove in a stew, they also cope with a far shorter session on the heat. These kebabs would be lovely eaten as a summer supper. If you wish, you can cut corners and buy the tzatziki ready-made.

2 x 275g lamb neck fillets
1½ teaspoons dried oregano
finely grated zest and juice of
   1 lemon
50ml olive oil
salt and black pepper

For the Greek salad:
2 teaspoons red wine vinegar
½ small garlic clove, peeled and
   finely chopped
4 tablespoons extra virgin olive oil
salt and pepper
450g vine-ripened tomatoes

½ cucumber, halved lengthways and
   de-seeded
1 small red onion, peeled and thinly
   sliced
50g small black olives
200g feta cheese, cubed
1–2 tablespoons fresh dill, chopped

For the tzatziki:
½ cucumber
200g Greek natural yogurt
2 garlic cloves, peeled and crushed
1 teaspoon lemon juice
1 tablespoon fresh mint, chopped
salt

For the lamb kebabs, cut the lamb into 3–4cm pieces, trimming away any excess fat. Put the meat into a bowl with the oregano, lemon zest and juice, oil and plenty of salt and pepper. Mix it all together well and leave it to get intimate at room temperature for an hour or so.

Now either light your barbecue or, when you're ready to eat, heat up a cast-iron griddle until it is smoking. Thread the meat onto 4 long meat skewers and brush the griddle, if that's what you are using, with a little oil. The meat will take around 12 minutes to cook on a medium heat, but keep an eye on them and turn them three or four times during cooking so that they are browned on all sides.

Meanwhile, prepare the salad and tzatziki. To make the Greek salad, put the vinegar, garlic, olive oil and some salt and pepper into a large salad bowl and whisk together. Just before you are ready to serve, add the tomatoes, cucumber, onion and olives and toss gently with the dressing. Add the feta cheese and dill and mix in with a light hand, taking care not to break up the delicate cheese.

To make the tzatziki, coarsely grate the cucumber, pile it onto a clean tea towel and squeeze out all the excess water. Mix in a bowl with the yogurt, garlic, lemon juice and mint and season with some salt to taste.

Serve all of the above together, and if there's some sun or a hint of warmth, the combination will transport you to an evening in a Greek tavern – plate-smashing is optional.

And after that …

I'm not one to bother with a dessert on a weekday, however, there are times when the midweek meal becomes unexpectedly celebratory. Someone might turn up with flowers or a particularly fine bottle of wine and, even though it's a Wednesday, it just feels right to prolong the evening and linger at the table. On such occasions the Vicar and I would opt for some good cheese over something sweet, but only if it's been bought from a shop that treats cheese with care. That means storing it at the perfect temperature (not fridge-cold but pretty darn chilly) and not introducing it to cling film or nasty vacuum wrap.

My favourite cheese treats

I know that I am spoiled, living in London, with a good selection of places where I can find cheese like this right on my doorstep. I lived in Borough for eight years and the temptation of Neal's Yard Dairy was something I inevitably failed to resist. I was always amazed at their passion for the stuff they were selling: not only would they offer you a taste of any cheese you asked about, they would mostly join in with the tasting, too. They knew if the Keen's Cheddar was currently superior to the Montgomery (in my mind, never); they knew which was the perfect goat's cheese to use in a tart. Dairy heaven.

Here, I share some of my very favourite cheeses. I offer them with suggestions for accompaniments, which could turn them into light meals in themselves, or else make them a fine way to finish one.

But don't let me to stop you going wild and buying more than one cheese: if you happen to get to Neal's Yard or your local equivalent cheese paradise, it would be awfully rude not to …

serves 2–4

Cashel Blue with pears

The Vicar doesn't like strong blue cheeses, but for him, this one makes the grade. It's almost-sweet saltiness and moist texture is perfect served with some lusciously ripe pears. To turn it into a meal, throw in some rocket and add a dressing emboldened with a smidgen of Dijon mustard.

Rosary Ash with cherries and thin organic oatcakes

This is one for me. I love this wonderful, fresh-tasting goat's cheese with its mysterious ashy coating. It is so light and zesty and so very, very easy to slip down. When it is spread on the earthy oatcakes and set off with sweet, plump cherries, this combination might be up there as my final snack, should I ever (which I sincerely hope I won't), end up on Death Row.

Montgomery Cheddar with Granny Smiths

In my first year of marriage I had bit of an addiction: cosied up on the sofa of an evening, I would find myself cutting up endless slices of apple and pieces of good Cheddar cheese. As soon as the Vicar and I had finished what was there, no, even before that, I would start slicing more. It took him telling me I had a problem to get me to stop. However, if I bought in some Montgomery, I think the Vicar might beg me to go back to my evil ways. Montgomery is the King of Cheddars, as far as he and I are concerned; its rich nuttiness is offset beautifully by sharply sweet apples. If there is any left over, serve it with an apple chutney with walnuts in it for an oh-so-simple, but utterly wonderful, lunch.

serves 2–4

Wigmore with raspberries

Wigmore is a sheep's cheese and its white milkiness wonderfully reminds you that this tasty little number came from something that said 'Baa'. Fragrantly floral, if you get hold of some in a young state, this cheese is offset beautifully by a punnet of sweet-sour raspberries. However, if this wonderful cheese is a little older and so has become more of a Brie, some wildly scented Muscatel grapes, dripping with desirable sweetness, will be just what you are after.

Comté with cornichons

It was some friends of ours, called the Moodys, who first introduced us to Comté cheese. They have the most inappropriate surname on the planet, as there couldn't be a less surly pair. Anyway, they arrived for dinner and kindly brought with them some delicious wine and this even more delicious cheese. It has an addictive sweetness, so accompanying it with the sharp cornichons (one of my particular loves and the only reason I might possibly be tempted by a Big Mac at McDonald's), works a treat.

Quick puddings for when the fancy takes you …

As I say, I haven't got a particularly sweet tooth, but I know some of you will. Here are some quick suggestions for those times when you don't want a precious evening to end, despite having to work the next day.

Lemon-curd Creams

8 tablespoons good-quality lemon
   curd
500g Greek yogurt

finely grated zest of 1 lemon, plus 2
   tablespoons juice
shortbread biscuits, to serve

In a bowl, mix together the lemon curd and the Greek yogurt, then add the lemon zest and juice. Spoon it out into individual serving bowls and serve with crisp shortbread biscuits.

This would also make a fabulous dip for fresh fruit, if you prefer.

serves 4

Summer Fruit Brûlée

500g summer berries (or use defrosted frozen fruit)

500g Greek yogurt or double cream caster sugar, for brûléeing

This recipe is a big fat cheat. Put the berries in a 1½-litre soufflé dish, or 4 large ramekins. Pour over the Greek yogurt or double cream, or a mixture of the two. Chill in the fridge for 1 hour. When you are ready to serve, sprinkle with enough sugar to cover the tops of the pudding, or puddings, and either caramelise it using a blow torch or under a hot grill.

Orange-scented Strawberries

500g strawberries
finely grated zest and juice of
  ¹⁄₂ orange
2 tablespoons icing sugar

2 tablespoons orange-flavoured
  liqueur, such as Cointreau
cream (single or double), to serve
  (optional)

Wash, hull and halve the strawberries and put them in a serving bowl. Stir in the orange zest and juice, and the icing sugar. Slosh in the orange-flavoured liqueur and chill for 1 hour in the fridge. Serve with cream, if you wish.

serves 4

Ricotta and Raspberries

This is such a simple, throw it all together recipe that the proportions of the ingredients are up to you – have as much of one and as little of another as you wish.

Divide among four servings plates a plump tump (in Wales, 'tump' means lots) of fresh ricotta cheese. Pour over a little single cream, sprinkle with caster sugar and surround it with raspberries.

Charentais and Stem Ginger

The Vicar's favourite melon combines well with that funny ginger you buy in jars. The only argument I'd have with the ludicrously talented Simon Hopkinson, is that the salmon dish with ginger and currants in his wonderful book, *Roast Chicken and Other Stories*, is just plain wrong. A talented cook once made it for us at our house and I was loath to say that I really wasn't impressed. Anyway, if you happen to have a jar of stem ginger that needs using, this makes a refreshing end to a meal.

Simply slice up some icily cold Charentais melon and scatter with some thinly sliced stem ginger and some of its syrup. Done.

Despite what they taught us at school, meals don't always have to be eaten at set times. Of course, eating three meals a day, as per tradition, is generally a good thing: it provides structure and routine and something to look forward to amongst all of life's stresses and strains. However, sometimes it feels right to rebel – to dispel ingrained behaviour and eat what you want, whenever you want. Give the Vicar and me a child-free Saturday (which is often gifted to us by my rather amazing out-laws), and he and I revel in throwing traditional foodie habits to the wind. A long, lazy brunch, or a lunch that fritters away the day, is the sort of stuff that injects some glitter into a weekend, and as we catch up on news and enjoy delicious food, we suddenly realise that the person we married is someone we actually love spending time with. Equally as pleasurable, albeit in a rather different way, are the times when dear, old friends, or the family, descend upon us. Suddenly the day becomes an open-ended, ongoing feast.

Some of the food in this chapter would make fabulous brunch fare to while away a weekend morning; other dishes could provide the necessaries for a lazy afternoon of picking at food. However, if, for you, these dishes cry out to be traditional lunches or a starter before a dinner party, please feel absolutely free to use them as such. I won't be in your house; and even if I was, I'd want to meet you and eat your food, not judge you. So, help yourself and use these dishes exactly how you please.

Flexible Food

Brunch

There is something both very soothing and utterly decadent about a long, leisurely mid-morning meal; the sort that takes place after a lazy lie-in and is assembled languorously once the friends have arrived. Lots of drinks are usually on offer: tea and coffee and fresh juices are on tap, and a Buck's Fizz or a Bloody Mary are always very welcome. There'll also be slices of melon and pineapple, lots of grapes and bowls of apples and pears.

My favourite sort of brunch is often one held after a party night, when everyone is a bit sleepy and keen to let the day drift by with idle chit-chat and ongoing grazing. On New Year's Day we do exactly that (see page 300 for brunch for a crowd), inviting over anyone who fancies putting off the harsh realities of January and a new year and prolonging the party spirit instead, albeit in a very gentle way. There's always an afternoon film on in the background, and people turn up as and when, and do as they please. One year one guest took this to the extreme and spent much of the afternoon under our bed, stroking/mauling our cat. The sight of his feet sticking out from under the bed rather scared a woman who had gone up to fetch her coat, but otherwise the Vicar and I had no objection to his behaviour whatsoever.

Houmous

This is Nadia's recipe, and when she served it it came with other delicious *meze*, followed by a traditional Palestinian wedding dish. With Middle Eastern music playing in the background and candles flickering, it was as though we'd been transported to a more exotic land.

This is delicious used to make the dressing to serve with the leg of lamb with cumin, lemon and mint on page 24, or you can use it as a dip for brunch.

1 x 400g tin chickpeas in brine
3 fat garlic cloves, peeled and
    crushed
7 tablespoons tahini paste (sesame
    seed paste)
juice of 1 large lemon, plus extra
    (optional)

salt and pepper
olive oil, for drizzling
toasted pine nuts, for sprinkling
warm pitta bread, to serve

Empty the tin of chickpeas into a pan and gently heat them for a couple of minutes. Drain, but reserve the liquid to use later. While the chickpeas are still hot, put them in a food processor with the crushed garlic, tahini paste, lemon juice and salt and pepper. Pulse the ingredients together, adding a little of the reserved chickpea liquid until the houmous has the consistency of mashed potato. Taste and add more seasoning or lemon juice, if you think it needs it. Smooth the houmous out onto 2 small plates, drizzle over a little olive oil and sprinkle with the toasted pine nuts. Eat with warm pitta bread and enjoy.

serves 10–12

An Un-fried Fry-up

This is a perfectly formed, guilt-free grill that's perfect when you have mixed company over: the boys get some of the greasy spoon components, and any weight-conscious girls can be content that they won't be eating grease. I serve mine with a big blob of brown sauce, but that's because, as the Vicar puts it, I'm a filthy peasant. And okay, before I start, let's get this straight: this is a simple dish, so you need top-notch ingredients. You know what I'm saying without me throwing in words like organic and butcher … Oh, but I just did.

4 large flat mushrooms
1 x 400g tin chopped tomatoes
15g butter
4 slices of rindless smoked back
   bacon

Worcestershire sauce
salt and pepper
4 large eggs

First, put the mushrooms in a shallow baking tray and season them liberally. Put them in a pre-heated oven at 200°C/Gas Mark 6. They'll be in there for about 20 minutes, so, in the meantime, pour the tomatoes into a pan, add salt and pepper and cook them over a low heat. You are aiming to not only heat them up but also to reduce the liquid a bit.

Put the water on for the eggs – either in a pan or, ideally, in an egg poacher. (The eggs have to play a balancing act in the final dish and the poacher will ensure a uniform shape that will make the assembly far easier.) If you do have a poacher, pop a knob of butter in each of the poaching things to melt. About 10 minutes before the mushrooms come out, preheat the grill and put the bacon on the rack of the grill pan. Put the bacon under the grill and cook lightly – you are not looking for crispy here.

When the bacon is ready, cut into small strips – I find this is easiest with some kitchen scissors – and add it to the tomatoes in the pan. Splash in 12–16 dashes of Worcestershire sauce and season with some salt and pepper. It should taste pretty punchy at this stage, but in the finished dish it will be toned down by the mushrooms and the eggs. Remove the mushrooms from the oven, and put them on either 2 or 4 warmed plates, depending on how many people you are serving.

Turn the oven down to its lowest setting and carefully spoon the tomato mixture into the mushrooms. Slip the plates back into the oven to keep warm; slide the eggs into the poacher; bang on the lid and cook for 3 minutes. Take the mushrooms out of the oven, and, using 2 dessertspoons, place an egg on each mushroom (they balance better upside down). Eat, maybe washed down with a big mug of builder's tea.

serves 2–4   An Un-fried Fry-up 215

De-constructed Eggs Royale

Eggs Royale is a fantastic dish, beloved by all. Here I give it a rather more delicate twist by serving it as a salad and including the carbohydrate content only in the form of a smattering of bagel croûtons. The result is decadence on a plate; the clean crispness of the little gem lettuces is offset by the richness of dolly-sized quails' eggs, smoked salmon and the eggy, creamy dressing. It would be perfect for a girly celebration brunch (Champagne obligatory). However, it would also be an appropriate dish to serve to a girl with a broken heart, dumped and, indeed, in the dumps, and so in need of love and the reassurance that, whatever the ex has told her, she is special, loved and worth splurging out for.

2 little gem lettuces, washed and chopped	For the dressing:
	2 egg yolks
125g smoked salmon (trimmings are fine)	1 teaspoon granulated sugar
	1 teaspoon English mustard
1 bagel	1 tablespoon white wine vinegar
8 quails' eggs	100ml double cream
	salt and pepper

Separate the little gem lettuces into leaves, wash and dry them well, then roughly tear them into smaller pieces. Put the lettuce in a large bowl and add the smoked salmon. Split the bagel in half, toast and then cut into 1cm squared croûtons. Bring a small pan of water to the boil and add the quails' eggs. Cook until they are softly set – not oozing gooey yolk, but not fully hard either – 2 minutes in the pan should do it. Then lift them out and plunge them into cold water to stop them cooking.

Whisk together the ingredients for the dressing, adding the cream and seasoning at the end. Peel and halve each quail's egg and add to the salad. Gradually mix in enough of the dressing to coat: you may not need all of it. Scatter over the croûtons and, before serving, open that Champagne.

Sausage Salad

This is joy on a plate, being both light and satisfying at the same time. It would make a great party brunch – just multiply the quantities according to how many will be at your table. If you want, you can ditch the potato and fry similar-sized cubes of bread, which will take only 10–15 minutes to cook. Or, as we did, have both.

2 medium floury maincrop
   potatoes, such as King Edwards
   or Maris Piper
5 tablespoons olive oil
salt and pepper
10 baby plum tomatoes

4 pork sausages
70g frilly lettuce, such as frisée
2 large eggs, at room temperature
1 tablespoon red wine vinegar
1 teaspoon French mustard

First, peel the potatoes and cut them into cubes of around 1cm square. If you want perfect squares, this may involve some potato wastage (sorry, Mum). Heat 2 tablespoons of the oil in a frying pan and fry the potatoes gently until cooked through – they should take around 20–25 minutes. When they're done, give them a good sprinkling of salt and set aside somewhere they can keep warm.

Meanwhile, pop the tomatoes into a shallow roasting tin drizzled with the remaining oil and some seasoning. Roast at 200°C/Gas Mark 6 – again, they'll take about 20 minutes. Preheat the grill to medium and bring a pan of water to the boil for the eggs. Grill the sausages for 8–10 minutes, turning now and then, until cooked through. Arrange the salad leaves on 2 plates. Put the eggs into the pan of boiling water and, once it has come back to the boil and is bubbling away furiously, turn the heat down and cook them for 4 minutes. When they are ready, plunge them into cold water, then peel them.

Take the tomatoes out of the oven and put them on a plate. Pour the tomato-scented oil from the tin into a small bowl and whisk in the vinegar, mustard and lots of salt and pepper. Use some of this to lightly dress the leaves; you won't need all of it, but the remainder will be handy for another salad. Now add the tomatoes, arrange the sausages (each cut in half lengthways) on top, as though they are the spokes of a wheel, and scatter over the fried potatoes. Finally, halve the eggs over each plate and place in the middle. Sprinkle them with a touch of pepper and salt, and you're done.

Soft-boiled Duck Eggs and Dippers

You don't have to use duck eggs here, but they do make the whole thing a bit more special. With their porcelain-white shells and buttercup-yellow yolks, they look so beautiful and taste rather richer and more luxurious than the eggs of the humble hen. You can track them down in farmers' markets, and Waitrose stock the ones from Clarence Court. My children love all eggs; however, it is a bit embarrassing when they ask me (loudly) in public whether they are having duck eggs, quails' eggs, or 'just' hens' eggs for tea. Honestly, how very ostentatious.

Per person:
1 or 2 duck eggs

For the dippers:
2–3 chipolata sausages

approx. 5 asparagus spears, trimmed
sliced good white bread for toast
 (about 2 slices)
butter for spreading
Gentleman's Relish, for spreading

Bring 2 pans of water to the boil, one with the addition of a little salt. Preheat the grill to medium. Put the sausages under the grill to cook, and lower the duck eggs into the pan of unsalted water. I have to admit that the only downside to duck eggs is that it is quite tricky to time their cooking perfectly. I love a soft yolk, and 6 minutes gave me that, although a section of the white was a bit watery. However, on my stove 7 minutes turned the yolks into firmer territory. So I plump for 6 minutes and put up with a bit of liquidy white.

When the sausages and eggs have both had 3 minutes, drop the asparagus into the pan of salted boiling water and cook until tender – about 3 minutes – then drain well. Meanwhile, make some toast, spread it with butter and Gentleman's Relish, and cut into fingers. Serve the eggs with the chipolatas, asparagus spears and fingers of toast, and make sure you've made a nice cup of tea.

Welsh Girl's Sausages

I might have lost my accent (I left Wales when I was only four) but I am not going to forget my roots. I was born in Caerphilly hospital, so these sausages are a tribute to this part of the world – and to my poor mother for giving birth to me. I am a heat-loving creature, and apparently I refused to come out of my warm cocoon for a very, very long time.

20g butter
1 leek, cleaned and finely chopped
200g fresh white breadcrumbs
175g Caerphilly cheese, grated
1½ tablespoons parsley, chopped

3 large eggs, lightly beaten
2 teaspoons Dijon mustard
3 tablespoons full-fat milk
salt and pepper
3 tablespoons sunflower oil

Melt the butter in a small pan, add the leek and fry lightly until softened. In a bowl, combine 150g of the breadcrumbs with the cheese, the leek, parsley and seasoning. Beat the eggs with the mustard and set aside 3 tablespoons of it in a flat bowl. Add the rest of the egg to the cheesy breadcrumb mixture and add a bit of the milk if it looks a bit dry (but stop before it gets all gloopy). Roll the mixture into sausage shapes, then dip them first into the reserved mustardy egg mixture and then into the remaining breadcrumbs. Pop them in the fridge to firm up for 30 minutes.

Heat the oil in a frying pan over a medium heat, add the sausages and fry for around 10 minutes, turning them now and then, until browned. Serve with grilled tomatoes, my rich tomato and harissa sauce (page 303), or, if brunch is slipping conveniently into lunchtime, a good tomato chutney. And, as any Welsh person might say: 'Now there's lovely, isn't it?'

serves 4

Soups and stocks

I've really changed my position on soup-making. Years ago, the thought of all that chopping put me off, and I also worried nervously about whether I was getting the quantities right, but nowadays, living with two small children who don't exactly hold back from making their needs felt, I find the chopping bit very calming. A bit like stirring a risotto, the whole process slows me down and prevents me from trying to do more than one thing at once. I have also abandoned all my fearful concerns about getting things wrong. You can't go *that* awry when combining some liquid and vegetables, surely? So while this section lists specific soup recipes, more often than not I tend to make soup when I have vegetables that need using up. It could be carrots, leeks, broccoli, or anything: I just throw in the pan what otherwise would end up in the bin.

Of course, a good stock helps; even if it is merely vegetable stock. I save every drop of water from when I boil my vegetables and either use it to cook with, or I drink it combined with Bovril so that none of the precious vitamins are poured down the sink (please feel free not to do this: I know it's slightly kooky, obsessive, and mad).

However, some soups demand a good chicken stock. Again, I used to find the whole business of making this frighteningly mysterious, but it's just about putting a few things in a big pan and letting them do their thing. The smell that emanates from a good chicken stock as it bubbles away on the stove, really is wondrously magical — even if you live in a sparse London loft, or a bed-sit in Bradford, your place will suddenly feel homely, full of welcome, solace and cosy warmth.

Chicken Stock

Yes, you can go and ask the butcher for bones, if that tickles your fancy; they'll probably be more than happy to throw them your way for a pittance. However, in our house, stock usually gets made after the Sunday roast chicken.

Simply strip the carcass of any remaining meat and put it in a covered bowl in the fridge. Break up the bird and put it in a large pan with various bits and bobs – a chopped carrot, a quartered onion, a bay leaf, a handful of black peppercorns, a good pinch of salt, a bit of parsley or thyme. Pour in 1.5 litres of cold water and bring to the boil. Skim off any scum that rises to the surface and reduce the heat. Cover and let the stock simmer away for a couple of hours or so. (If you wish, you can leave it longer, allowing the stock to reduce still further. This is ideal if you want to freeze it, as it will take up less freezer space. You could even reduce it right down and freeze it in ice cubes. Then, when you want to use it, you just need to add more water to bring it back to a classic stock strength.)

Strain the cooked stock into a bowl and allow to cool. When it is cold, skim off any fat with a spoon. The stock will keep in the fridge for a week or in the freezer for a couple of months.

makes about 1.5 litres

Butternut Buttercup Soup

This soup is so lovely, so hugely cheering. Not only is it good for you, but it's also satisfying and richly fragrant. Yes, the ingredients are found easily, come the autumn, but it also brings back the memory of warmer days. I promise you, the finished soup is the colour of buttercups warmed by the sun.

2 tablespoons olive oil
1 onion, peeled and finely chopped
1 garlic clove, peeled and crushed
1 large butternut squash, peeled and
    cut into 2cm chunks
1.2 litres hot vegetable stock (fresh,
    or use a good-quality liquid
    bouillon), or hot water
salt and pepper

5 yellow or orange peppers
a small chunk of Chèvre cheese, a
    couple of basil leaves and a
    drizzle of olive oil, preferably
    infused with basil, to serve (all
    optional, but they really do lift
    the soup out of the ordinary and
    make it sing)

In a large pan, heat the oil and sauté the onion and garlic until they are softened but not brown – about 5 minutes. Add the chopped squash, stir in with the onion and cook for around 5 minutes more, before adding the hot stock or water. Bring it to the boil and season with salt and pepper. Then turn down the heat, put a lid on the pan and let it all bubble away for 20–25 minutes or until the squash is soft.

Meanwhile, cut the peppers in half lengthways, de-seed them and place them, skin-side up, under a hot grill until the skins are black and charred. When they are cool enough not to burn your fingers off, peel away the skins and, using your trusty kitchen scissors, snip strips of the peppers into the soup.

serves 4

Blend thoroughly (I use my hand-held blender here, much less bother than getting out your food processor). Test for seasoning, adding more salt and pepper if necessary, and serve with the goat's cheese, basil leaves and oil floating attractively on the surface.

Celery Soup with Fourme d'Ambert and Pancetta Croûtons

This is a rich, luxurious soup, so you don't need lots of it per person. It would make a decadent starter for the winter months, or it would be equally perfect served for lunch during the festive season with a glass of flinty white wine and some good bread. I love Fourme d'Ambert obsessively, but you could use a different blue cheese if you can't find it. Just make sure you go for something not too strong, like Cashel Blue. You aren't after the salty hit of Stilton here, but something rather more mellow.

50g butter
1 onion, peeled and finely chopped
2 heads of celery, leaves on, finely
   chopped
1.5 litres water

200ml single cream
120g Fourme d'Ambert cheese,
   crumbled
150g cubed pancetta
salt and pepper

Melt the butter and stir in the onion and celery (including the leaves) to soften – 5 minutes should do it. Add the water and cook away gently for about 20 minutes, lid on. Remove the lid, turn up the heat and let it bubble away a bit, reducing the liquid by a third. Add the cream and the cheese and season. Keep tasting it until you're happy. Blend the soup with a hand-held blender or in a food processor.

In the meantime, pop the pancetta into a frying pan without any oil and brown it over a medium heat: you don't want it burnt, just crisping up. To serve, gently heat the soup through again and scatter the pancetta 'croûtons' on top of the delicious celery creaminess.

serves 4–6

Leek Soup with Cashel Blue Croûtes

Whilst leek and potato soup is ubiquitous, a soup that sings purely in praise of the leek is a rare thing. Here, the leek's sweetness is brought out by the contrast of salty cheese. I am sorry to be bossily specific about which one I'd go for, but the man I married only likes creamier blues. It is pure serendipity that with this soup, such a cheese is the perfect partner: neither overpowering nor fading, uncomfortable and apologetic, into the background. A bit like the man I married, in fact.

This soup would make a lovely Saturday lunch, but we ate it with friends on a cold Saturday night, eyes glued to the box.

75g butter

1kg leeks (that's about 8 leeks), cleaned and chopped

200ml white wine

1 litre chicken stock (fresh, or use a good-quality liquid bouillon), or water

100ml single cream

salt and pepper

6 slices of baguette

6 thick slices of Cashel Blue cheese, or something similarly blue, mild and creamy

Melt the butter in a large pan and stir in the leeks. Cook them over a low heat for about 15 minutes or until soft. Now add all the wine and the stock or water and turn up the heat. Bring to the boil, lower the heat slightly and let it bubble away and reduce a bit. Finally, add the cream and some seasoning. The soup now needs a thoroughly good blitz in a food processor or liquidiser to acquire a fairly smooth consistency.

When you are ready to serve, preheat the grill to high. Put the slices of baguette onto the rack of the grill pan and toast on both sides. Take them out, put a slice of cheese on top of each one and pop the bread under the grill again until the cheese is a picture of molten, bubbling loveliness. Serve the croûtes floating in the soup.

Salads

Salads have come a long way since the 80s. I remember dreadful Sunday afternoon teas of wet iceberg lettuces, hard, unripe tomatoes and slimy ham served with the ubiquitous dollop of Heinz salad cream. Come the noughties, however, and salads have grown up. It's as though they've been to see a careers adviser who's alerted them to all they really have to offer. No longer do they loiter, unnoticed, on the side of the plate; instead they proudly take centre stage. At least, they do in my house.

I don't just reserve salads for summer, either. Whilst in summer my salads will look fresh and fragrant, my winter ones are usually warm, but with a bit more weight to them. Even then, the Vicar fails to be totally convinced: on salad days at our house, you may find him in the caff next door, eating a manly sized plate of sausage, egg and chips.

A Pretty Pink Salad

This is fabulously girly and definitely cries out for pink fizz. Light and refreshing, this one is best eaten in the summer, and would also make a charming starter.

10 radishes, finely sliced
4 spring onions, finely chopped
1 baby gem lettuce, chopped
100g smoked salmon trimmings
6 sprigs of dill
$^1/_2$ lemon, quartered
fresh baguette and butter, to serve

For the dressing:
2 tablespoons extra virgin olive oil
1 tablespoon lemon oil
1 tablespoon lemon juice
1 small teaspoon French mustard
salt and pepper

This is so easy. All you do is combine the first 4 ingredients in a shallow salad bowl, then make the dressing by whisking together the oils, lemon juice, mustard and seasoning. Add the dressing to the bowl and toss the salad together. Garnish with the dill sprigs and the lemon quarters and serve with slices of a fresh baguette and some good butter.

serves 2

Hot Halloumi Salad

Halloumi is like meat: it's not meant to be eaten uncooked. After a few minutes on the grill, however, the cheese becomes delectably savoury, melting and, yes, kind of meaty. That's why this recipe is a bit of a crowd-pleaser: it's great for vegetarians, but somehow the halloumi satisfies even the most dedicated of carnivores. (One for the Vicar, then …)

5 medium plum tomatoes, quartered
1 x 10cm chunk of cucumber, cut into small dice
½ little gem lettuce, chopped
1 tablespoon coriander, chopped
1 tablespoon basil leaves, torn up
2 spring onions, white part only, finely chopped
a little olive oil, for oiling the griddle pan
250g halloumi cheese (or 1 packet)

1 teaspoon red chilli (fresh or 'Lazy Chilli' from a jar), de-seeded and finely chopped
salt and pepper

For the dressing:
3 tablespoons extra virgin olive oil
juice of ½ lime
salt and pepper
a little red chilli (fresh or 'Lazy Chilli' from a jar), de-seeded and finely chopped, to taste

In an ideal world, take a big, shallow, white salad bowl. If you don't have one, use something similar and comfort yourself with the fact that you can't expect life to be perfect all the time. To your bowl, add the first 6 ingredients, then make up the dressing. Whisk together the extra virgin olive oil, the lime juice and salt and pepper – going easy on the salt as the cheese has lots of its own. Now you need to add some chilli. I have two big problems with chilli: the first is that everyone likes a different amount of it; the second, that I inevitably rub my eyes when chopping chilli. So, C-grader chef that I am, I take the easy route. I buy a jar of 'Lazy Chilli' (please don't tell anyone) and to the dressing I add $\frac{1}{2}$ teaspoon of this ready-made eye-saver. If you are an expert in the chilli-slicing department, ignore all my below-par pointers and revel in your chilli-chopping prowess. Reserve about 2 teaspoons of the dressing and add the rest to the salad, and toss.

Lightly oil a ridged, iron griddle pan, or frying pan, until it's smoking hot. Slice the halloumi widthways into about 10 pieces. Taking a teaspoon, dip it into the chilli jar and smear a bit of chilli onto each slice of cheese. Now stick your fingers right in the chilli jar and rub thoroughly into both eyes … (Sorry, that bit was a joke.)

Cook the cheese on both sides for about 3 minutes or until soft and brown-edged. Add the cooked cheese slices to the salad immediately: some mixed in and some arranged temptingly on the top. Drizzle with the reserved dressing and eat as soon as it hits the table.

serves 2

Hot Halloumi Salad   233

Warm Chorizo, Feta and Cherry Tomato Salad

I have two Irish friends both called Helen, and this recipe comes from one of them. Fluent in Spanish and, like me, a lover of Spain: its cities, its countryside, its people and its food, Helen made this as a starter once when she was round at my house. While she stood at the stove looking utterly relaxed, twelve of us sat in the garden, quaffing Rioja, the candles flickering in the fading light. The dish is far, far more than the sum of its parts: the gutsy chorizo set off by the salty feta and sweet tomatoes, all brought together by the addition of red wine that absorbs all the flavours and cries out for pieces of bread for dunking.

1 chorizo (*del pueblo* is lovely in this
   dish)
1 tablespoon olive oil
16 cherry tomatoes, halved

175ml red wine
200g feta cheese, cubed
salt and pepper

Cut the chorizo into even-sized chunks – everyone should have about 4 chunks each. Heat the oil in a large frying pan and sauté the chunks until lightly browned and hot. Throw the tomatoes in the pan and toss them around until soft. Pour in the wine and allow it to bubble and reduce by about half, before adding in the feta and stirring gently to combine everything. Season with lots of freshly ground black pepper and a touch of salt to taste. Serve in a huge bowl for people to pass round, with hunks of bread for mopping up the juices.

see page 200

Lamb Kebabs with Greek Salad and Tzatziki

Italian Polpette

see page 195

see page 195

Italian Polpette

Soft-boiled Duck Eggs and Dippers see page 220

see page 231

Radishes for a Pretty Pink Salad

Spanish Tapas

see page 269

see page 269

Spanish Tapas

Lobster, King Prawn and Mango Salad

see page 280

Herbaceous Smoked Haddock

This is a satisfying main-course salad, perfect for when you want salad and sustenance on the same plate. Salad as comfort food: now, that's a new idea.

4 new potatoes, washed or scraped, then halved

300g undyed smoked haddock

1 red onion, peeled

12 baby plum tomatoes, halved

1 tablespoon olive oil

150g mixed salad leaves (watercress, spinach and rocket would be perfect)

1 tablespoon flatleaf parsley, chopped

1 tablespoon dill, chopped

a large handful of sugar snap peas

For the dressing:

2 tablespoons crème fraîche

2 tablespoons wholegrain mustard

1 tablespoon white wine vinegar

salt and pepper

Preheat the oven to 180°C/Gas Mark 4. The potatoes and haddock both take 20 minutes to cook, so prepare them together. Put the potatoes in a pan of boiling, salted water and wrap your haddock in foil. Pop the fish on a baking tray and bake it in the oven.

Whilst these two are doing their thing, slice the red onion into fine rings. (It's quite important you make them *fine* rings, as you are going to grill them, and hot, thick onion rings only serve to remind me of burger vans – which isn't the feel you're after here, at all.) Add the halved tomatoes to the onion rings on a baking tray and drizzle with the olive oil. Cook under a hot grill for 5 minutes until soft and slightly browned here and there.

Get out your favourite big bowl and toss in the salad leaves and finely chopped herbs. In a small bowl, whisk together the ingredients for the dressing. About 2 minutes before the potatoes are ready, add the sugar snaps to the pan with them. Once the 2 minutes are up, drain the vegetables and put back into the hot pan with enough of the dressing to coat.

Take the haddock out of the oven, check it's cooked (it should be opaque all the way through and flake easily), and remove the skin. Break into large flakes, discarding any bones, and add to the salad along with the vegetables in their dressing. Toss everything together, being careful not to break up the fish, and add more of the dressing. (You probably won't need all of it: you want the salad to be well dressed, not drowning.) Finally, scatter the grilled onion and the tomatoes over the top of the salad, serve, and eat.

Puttanesca Plate

This salad is based on the pasta sauce of the same name. I won't remind you what the translation is in English; I'm far too polite. Oh, go on then, force me. It means 'prostitute'. There, I've said it. Anyway, it's a salad where the colours are bright, the flavours assertive, and I think it would be perfect (despite its unbefitting name) to serve a girlfriend who has fallen madly in love.

Most girls attest that, when love's arrow has entered the heart, all appetite for solid food is quelled. So, if your visiting friend is lovesick, my prescription would be to serve up a few vibrant little plates of food, tapas-style. You never know, it may tempt the poor thing into grazing. However, if none of your friends has gone all gooey over someone, this dish would make a very good starter, or an accompaniment for something grilled, such as tuna, salmon, or even chicken.

3 heaped tablespoons flatleaf parsley, chopped
8 baby plum tomatoes, halved
10 good-quality pitted black olives from the deli counter, not a tin
1 spring onion, finely chopped or ¼ red onion, finely chopped
1 tablespoon capers, rinsed in cold water and drained

10–12 fresh white anchovies (you can get them on any good deli counter)
salt and pepper
a few drizzles of lemon oil (or just use extra virgin olive oil if you don't have any)

serves 2

This salad is basically an assembly job. On a plate or in a shallow salad bowl, layer the parsley, tomatoes, olives, onion and, finally, the capers. Arrange the fresh white anchovies (you really don't want the tinned kind) on top of the salad in a wheel effect. (I would be nibbling on these as I put the salad together, as they are one of my favourite things in the world. My friend Pete feels the same, but unfortunately for him, he now lives in the States and our favourite little fishies are impossible to track down anywhere over there.) Add salt and pepper and a few drizzles of lemon oil.

Hand food

By hand food I don't mean finger food of the sort that is eaten decorously at elegant parties; no indeed, hand food is altogether more earthy. This is the kind of stuff that's normally eaten on the run when your hunger is just too great to wait for the meal to come. Most often it is grabbed with little or no thought from the newsagent's for 50p, from the biscuit tin in the cupboard, or from the local shop in a cellophane pack. Laden with sugar or salt, they are the drugs of the food world: they lift you up and then, when the hit has faded, you're left feeling worse than ever. Now, I'm not saying you should never eat crisps or chocolate biscuits or cheese pasties ever again, it's just that we can do ourselves a big favour by cutting out such junk and grabbing a banana instead.

However, the fact is, sometimes we just can't do it. When the Vicar is on the sofa watching a rugby match, or when we are curled up watching a DVD or an episode of *The West Wing*, a banana doesn't really cut the mustard in the hand-food stakes. So, for those times, here are my offerings; much more interesting, tastier and healthier than what lies beneath any cellophane wrapping.

Lincolnshire meets Lancashire Sausage Rolls

There is no point eating sausages unless they are made with love. Oh, and lots of good pork. I'm lucky: I have a fabulous butcher just up the road and when I serve their sausages there are always 'oohs' and 'aaahs'. You can tell after one mouthful that you aren't eating any of the rubbish stuff that lurks beneath all too many sausage skins. For ages, my cousin pleaded with her husband to agree to move into my neighbourhood; and for just as long he refused. However, one fine day, a taste of these sausages and a visit to the cheese shop was enough to win him round: they now live round the corner.

The Lincolnshire version of my butcher's beauties are ideal in this recipe; their tasty porkiness is set off by salty Lancashire cheese and the sweetness of apple chutney. I don't usually go for sausage rolls, but made with the filo pastry, these are far lighter than the usual kind. They'd make a great lunch with a salad and maybe some coleslaw and a beer.

Per roll, which serves 1–2:
4 sheets of fresh, ready-made filo pastry
30g butter, melted (you may not need all of it)
Lancashire cheese, coarsely grated (be as generous as you like)
1 tablespoon good-quality apple chutney (mine was from my cheese shop and also had walnuts in)
2 Lincolnshire pork sausages, the best you can find

Brush 1 sheet of filo pastry with some of the melted butter and place on a baking tray, which has also been brushed with some of the butter. Brush the filo pastry with more melted butter and lay over a second sheet and brush with more butter. Cover with a third sheet, brush with more butter, then scatter over some cheese to cover the pastry. Add the final sheet of filo pastry then scatter more cheese on top of that. Spread over enough chutney to coat the pastry. Take the sausages out of their skins, roll them into one long, thin sausage and position it lengthways down the centre of the pastry. Fold the shorter sides of the pastry over the ends of the sausage and then roll it up into 1 large sausage roll. Brush with the remaining butter. Bake for around 30 minutes at 200°C/Gas Mark 6, or until the filo pastry has browned and the sausage is cooked through (stick the end of a sharp knife in the middle to check). See below for some other tasty variations.

venison or beef sausages with Stilton and cranberry sauce
This version would be lovely around Christmas time, maybe on Boxing Day while watching a film. Just follow the instructions above and swap the cheeses and chutneys. Make sure the Stilton is finely crumbled, though.

Welsh girl's sausages with tomato chutney
This variation incorporates the sausages from the recipe on page 222. Here, you dispense with the need for any cheese-sprinkling, as it's already in the sausages. I'd be happy without the filo pastry, but if you have some rogue vegetarians present, it's good to give everyone what *looks* like the same thing.

serves 1–2   Lincolnshire/Lancashire Sausage Rolls   241

Vietnamese Prawn Wraps

I love the fragrant lightness of Vietnamese food. We have a place just up the road that does take-away food, and I love getting a group of mates round and ordering lots of things to share. It's a rare thing to eat a take-away and feel virtuous afterwards, but every time we have ordered in, everyone comments that this is exactly how they feel.

The recipe here is my approximation of one of their dishes. It makes a big bowl of prawn salad, which would be lovely eaten as such. However, I recommend you get hold of some Vietnamese rice papers (Sharwoods make them, or else buy them online from somewhere like www.orientalmart.co.uk.). With a match to watch and a beer in hand, this makes a lovely snack to assemble and to relish, guilt-free.

This recipe would make around 30 rolls (but don't take me to the stake over it – it was a relaxed evening and some of us just dug in to the salad). But, hey, make it, and tell me if I'm wrong …

200g large (not king) cooked
  prawns, peeled, or cooked chicken
125g Cos lettuce, finely shredded
8cm piece of cucumber, peeled, de-
  seeded and shredded lengthways
2 large carrots, peeled and coarsely
  grated
4 spring onions, cut into 4 and
  finely shredded lengthways
50g roasted peanuts, roughly
  chopped
1 tablespoon each basil, mint and
  coriander, chopped

30 Vietnamese rice papers (about
  3–4 per person)
sweet chilli sauce, for dipping
  (optional)

For the dressing:
1 garlic clove, peeled and crushed
1 red chilli, de-seeded and finely
  chopped
1 tablespoon caster sugar
juice of 2 limes
3 tablespoons Thai fish sauce

Put all the salad ingredients in a large salad bowl and toss together (except the rice papers and sweet chilli sauce). Whisk together the ingredients for the dressing in a small bowl and set both aside. The rice papers just need to be put in very hot water to soften up. Read the instructions on your particular packet, but it will usually be a matter of $\frac{1}{2}$–1 minute or so before they plump up. Do them a few at a time, lift them out of the water and place them on a clean tea towel to drain, then transfer them to a serving dish.

To serve, toss the dressing through the salad and instruct your guests to place some of the salad down the centre of each rice paper and roll up. If you are a chilli freak, feel free to serve some sweet chilli sauce on the side for dipping into.

makes around 30 rolls   Vietnamese Prawn Wraps   243

A good plate of sandwiches

Gone are the days when the only place you'd find a take-away sandwich was the likes of Greggs or, where I grew up, the Baker's Oven. I remember, as a sixth-former, feeling so grown up to be allowed out at midday to buy my own lunch. Oh, the intoxicating thrill of waiting in the queue for a cheese and tomato bap while my friend was up the street somewhere else, gleefully getting a chip buttie for 80p. Meanwhile, the Vicar, down south, was loafing around Guildford, wondering which girl from his school would like to be bought an egg roll. A nasty thought. These days, however, sandwiches have gone all posh. You see people standing in one of the umpteen sandwich shops, in delis or high-class supermarkets, spending half their lunch hour agonising about whether to have the crayfish and rocket in granary or the sunblush tomato, mozzarella and avocado. Sometimes, so hard is the choice, they give up and just walk out. Or maybe that's just me.

I think it is because the sandwich world has become so smart (and expensive with it) that we don't take much care if we make one ourselves. Sure, we might slip a bit of cheese between two slices of white plastic bread and eat it standing up in the kitchen; heck, we might even throw in a few slices of tomato; but we hardly ever make sandwiches with love. Shamed by the plethora of designer sandwiches in every shop we go in, we have lost our own sandwich imagination: it doesn't feel worth the effort.

May I make a plea for us to throw down the gauntlet and challenge the sandwich shops? Making your own is, overall, cheaper than buying one – even if you use upmarket ingredients. Added to that, you will know exactly what's in it; you can choose whether you want butter or mayonnaise, and whether you want to include salad. And when friends ask: 'Wow, where did you get that?', you can smugly reply, 'Actually, I made it myself.'

You can make any of these sandwiches to consume alone, for lunch in the office, or at home. I've included a few tips to make sure you don't get bored and either end up eating a particular sandwich all week, or just wasting food. Or, for a shared sandwich experience, why not invite a group of friends for a civilised tea one day? I promise they'll be impressed.

All sandwiches make enough for one – that's a baguette or roll or 2 rounds of bread. I have neither listed ingredients (there aren't very many) nor quantities – I think sandwiches are very much a matter of personal taste. Indeed, if I list something you would prefer to leave out, feel totally free to do so. It's your sandwich, after all.

Wensleydale, Apricot Chutney and Watercress Sandwich

I am a chutney and pickle fanatic – and not just at Christmas. As a child, cheese sandwiches weren't worth eating without the Branston. As an adult, I haven't exactly moved on from my chunky brown friend, but my tastes are wider. The problem is that more unusual chutney, although lovingly acquired, often ends up lurking sulkily at the back of the cupboard, wondering why, after the initial fuss and excitement of being brought home, it isn't getting any attention. I have to admit it is sometimes hard to know what to do with these precious jars of tastiness; you can't exactly eat chutney by itself for breakfast. However, sandwiches are an ideal solution. In this Wensleydale number, the salty cheese, traditionally served with heady pear, is offset by sweet apricot. And the watercress adds a nice dose of pepper.

Spread 2 slices of bread with butter – I recommend a nice crusty white here. Spread one side of the bread with chutney, sprinkle over as much crumbled cheese as you fancy, and scatter over some watercress. Pop the other slice of bread on the top, press down, and cut in half.

other ideas for Wensleydale

Cut a pear into quarters and pan fry in a little butter. Make some cheese on toast with the Wensleydale and serve with the pear.

Use in place of Lincolnshire cheese in the sausage rolls on page 240.

Make a coleslaw of grated carrot, onion, white cabbage, grated pear, raisins and Wensleydale. It will need a French dressing of three parts olive oil to one of white wine vinegar, a smidgen of French mustard, a crushed garlic clove and some salt and pepper.

King Prawn, Mango Chutney and Bacon Sandwich

Another day and, for me, another chutney. This combination works because the charm of cold, unanointed king prawns lies chiefly in their texture; there is something very satisfying about biting into their firm flesh. The chutney adds fruity feistiness to the sandwich; the bacon, meaty depth. Again, I would use white bread: the bacon told me to tell you it won't lie next to anything else.

Spread some mayonnaise thinly on both slices of bread, then top with thinly smeared mango chutney. Fry 2 slices of unsmoked bacon until fairly crisp. Scatter some prawns over the first slice of bread, top with some softly flavoured salad leaves from a bag, then lay over the bacon and the other slice of bread. There, you're done.

other ideas for prawns

Make a good, old-fashioned prawn cocktail. Either use a shop-bought seafood sauce or make it yourself and give yourself a shock as to how it is made (you may never want to eat it again). In a bowl, combine an equal amount of salad cream and mayonnaise and then stir in enough tomato ketchup to turn it a pink seafood-sauce colour (see, I told you it would put you off). Add a dash of Tabasco and lemon juice and some salt and pepper, stir, then throw in enough cooked peeled prawns to be fully coated in the sauce. Shred some lettuce leaves (use whatever you have to hand) and put them at the bottom of a bowl (preferably a glass one from the 70s) and pile over the prawns. Add a shaking of paprika and eat with brown bread and butter. Preferably wearing flares.

serves 1

Make an omelette: First, cut some cooked, peeled tiger prawns in half, or even in thirds, as otherwise they will feel too much of a chewy mouthful in such a delicate dish. Now melt 1 teaspoon of butter and the same of oil in a small frying pan. Lightly beat together 3 large eggs with some seasoning until frothy, and, when the fat is foaming, pour in the eggs, tilting the pan to spread everything. Keep lifting up the edges of the omelette to allow the still-liquid egg to slip underneath what is already set. When the omelette is almost cooked, toss 1 tablespoon of chopped chives over the top, along with 50g of diced goat's cheese. Finally, add the prawns and, when the omelette looks set all over, fold and serve. I am sure Elizabeth David would approve if, at this point, you poured yourself a nice glass of white wine.

An Asian omelette: In a bowl, lightly mix together 3 large eggs, 1 teaspoon of sesame oil, 2 teaspoons of light soy sauce, 2 crushed garlic cloves and 1 teaspoon of crushed ginger. Heat 1 tablespoon of vegetable or sunflower oil in a small frying pan until it is spitting, then pour in the egg mixture. Stir lightly to set, moving the set egg to allow the runny egg to slide underneath. When the omelette is set, scatter over 1 tablespoon of chopped fresh coriander and either 1 tablespoon of bean sprouts or chopped spring onions. Finally, arrange a handful of thinly sliced, cooked, peeled tiger prawns down the middle of the omelette and fold. Serve with some sort of dipping sauce: oyster sauce mixed with soy, sweet chilli sauce or plum.

Sit down with a good book or a film and eat the prawns as they are, dipped into garlic mayonnaise.

Hot Mushroom, Stilton and Lamb's Lettuce Sandwich

I include this one out of a sense of nostalgia. Many years ago I was doing a pretty awful temping job in Bristol, the only upside being the fact I was living near my boyfriend/future husband, who was working in Human Resources at the time. One lunchtime he spontaneously picked me up in his very unglamorous, mustard-coloured Cavalier, armed with this sandwich, which he'd bought at work. We sat and ate on a rather gritty verge by the side of the road, cars racing past us. True romance.

This sandwich is best eaten warm and, again, unhealthy girl that I am, I would plump for white bread. Some sort of doughy white bap would be nice – this, along with the lamb's lettuce (or another soft-flavoured salad leaf, like baby spinach) softens and tempers what are quite strong flavours.

You can use either 1 big portabella mushroom or 8 chestnut mushrooms. In either case, slice finely and fry in a small knob of butter (about 2 teaspoons) and 2 teaspoons of olive oil. Meanwhile, crumble or slice about 30g of Stilton (but, really, how much you use is your business and will depend on the size of the bap you are using). When the mushrooms are cooked and brown, but still soft, add a little seasoning. Slice the bap in half and drizzle the pan juices over both halves of the bread. Put the mushrooms on one side of the bap, scatter over the cheese and, finally, a handful of the salad leaves. Close the bap and devour, preferably not at the side of a busy road.

other ideas for Stilton

Use in the venison, Stilton and cranberry sausage rolls on page 241.

Make a creamy Stilton sauce for chicken, steak or a baked potato. Pour around 125ml cream into a pan and heat until very hot, then crumble in around 50g Stilton. Stir until melted and hot, then season to taste with black pepper.

Make a salad: Cut 2 or 3 slices of smoked streaky bacon into strips with kitchen scissors and fry them in 2 tablespoons of olive oil until as brown and as crisp as you like it. Meanwhile, cover a plate with salad leaves and as much cubed Stilton as you fancy. You could also add cherry tomatoes or sliced pear. When the bacon is ready, add it to the salad using a slotted spoon, and then put the pan back on the stove. Pour in either 2 teaspoons of balsamic vinegar or sherry vinegar, a scant teaspoon of French mustard and lots of black pepper. It will steam and hiss and look very cross, but don't be afraid. Gradually pour the dressing onto the salad, tossing the leaves to see if it needs more lubricant. If it does, add a drizzle of extra virgin olive oil. When the leaves are glossy and nicely coated, throw aside the frying pan and enjoy a solitary treat.

serves 1

Smoked Trout with Horseradish Mayonnaise and Chives Sandwich

Finally, a sandwich that requires brown bread. This little darling is quite elegant; perfect for serving at an afternoon tea along with other dainty morsels and a large pot of perfectly brewed tea. Smoked trout is very delicate and softly spoken, so it is rather surprising that the inclusion of punchy horseradish does not overpower, but rather brings out the beauty of this lovely fish. (See page 90 for a hot version of this wonderful combination.)

In a bowl combine 2 teaspoons (or maybe more) of horseradish sauce with 1 tablespoon of mayonnaise and maybe a dash of double cream. I am sorry if these quantities are loose, but it is just that all horseradish sauces are not made equal; some are quite mild, others extremely hot; so taste what you have made, after adding a squeeze of lemon juice and a little salt and pepper. If the sauce is too hot, add more mayonnaise, and if you want more bite, reach for the horseradish. Finally, add 2 teaspoons of chopped chives. Feel free to double these quantities if you are making lots of sandwiches. Flake 1 or 2 hot-smoked trout fillets, depending on how many sandwiches you are serving, and combine it with the horseradish mayonnaise. Take your brown bread and plonk 1 tablespoon of the trout mixture on one side of the bread and spread it out. Decide if you want a bit more and then, when you are happy, cover with the other slice of bread. If you are aspiring to elegance, remove the crusts and cut the sandwiches into dainty quarters.

serves 1

other ideas for smoked trout and horseradish mayonnaise

Boil some new potatoes (ideally some Jersey Royals, if they are in season), and serve with the sauce. Or pile the trout into a buttery baked potato, maybe with a little salad to add a touch of green crispness.

For a hot version of your sandwich, pile the trout on a slice of brown toast and grill until bubbling.

If you have some horseradish mayonnaise left over when making this sandwich and you happen to come by some rare, thinly sliced, cold roast beef, it's time to make another sandwich. Rye bread would be nice here, but neither would I say no to that white crusty favourite of mine. Ah, the endless possibilities of the humble sandwich …

Sweet treats

I confess I'm not much of a baker and I do far prefer savoury snacks to sweet. However, sometimes the smell of freshly cooked biscuits is the just the thing to inject your house with the kind of homely warmth you used to feel at Granny's. And if you happen to live with any small (or even not so small) children, making sugar-scented treats is a great way to keep them occupied on a rainy afternoon.

Toasted Marshmallow and Chocolate Biscuit 'Sandwiches'

Easy as pie, these. Healthy they certainly are not, but for an occasional splurge, totally justifiable.

Thread 3 marshmallows onto 6 thin, wet, metal skewers and toast them over a naked gas flame until tinged golden brown all over. Slide them off the skewers with a fork while hot, and sandwich them between chocolate-coated biscuits (milk-chocolate Hob-Nobs are particularly good), chocolate sides facing inwards. Squeeze together gently, dust with icing sugar and serve for a squidgy chocolate fix.

Cranberry, Blueberry, Apple and Coconut Flapjacks

Packed with enough oats and fruit to rival a wholefood shop, you'd swear these were totally virtuous.

200g unsalted butter, plus extra for greasing
100g golden syrup
100g light soft brown sugar
finely grated zest of 1 orange
$1/4$ teaspoon salt
350g rolled porridge oats

100g dried apple rings, roughly chopped
100g dried cranberries
100g dried blueberries
100g flaked coconut
75g pumpkin seeds

Preheat the oven to 160°C/Gas Mark 3 and grease a shallow, 25cm square tin with butter.

Put the butter, golden syrup, sugar and orange zest together in a pan and warm gently until the butter and sugar have melted. Mix all the other ingredients together in a large bowl, add the melted ingredients and stir together well. Using the back of a wet tablespoon, press the mixture evenly over the base of the tin. Bake for 20 minutes or until lightly browned on top. Leave to go cold, then cut into rectangular pieces.

makes 6

Peanut Butter Cookies

Peanut butter divides people as strongly as Marmite. The Vicar can't stand the stuff, whereas I have a secret jar I dip into when my energy levels are flagging. I know eating it straight out of the pot isn't a very appealing habit, but there are worse ones I could mention …

175g butter, plus extra for greasing (if needed)
100g organic crunchy peanut butter
100g caster sugar
100g demerara sugar
225g plain flour
$\frac{1}{4}$ teaspoon salt

Preheat the oven to 200°C/Gas Mark 6. Cream the butter and peanut butter together in a bowl with a hand-held electric mixer. Stir in the caster and demerara sugar, followed by the flour and salt. Bring the mixture together into a ball and then divide into approximately 32 even-sized pieces. Roll each piece into a ball (children will enjoy this bit) and place them well-spaced apart on a lightly greased or non-stick baking sheet.

Flatten very slightly with the palm of your hand, then make a criss-cross pattern in the top of each one with the back of a small sharp knife. Bake in the oven for 12–15 minutes until richly golden. Remove from the oven and leave to cool on the tray for about 5 minutes or until firm enough to move, then transfer them to a cooling rack and, if possible, eat ever so slightly warm, maybe with a glass of milk.

makes about 32

The Great Chocolate Rescue Remedy

Finally, a little something for the ladies; or rather, ladies at a certain time of the month. We all know what it's like: PMT strikes and overnight we turn from rational, relaxed, sunny creatures to erratic, grumpy monsters. At times like this there's only one thing for it: chocolate. This recipe delivers what you need in spades, and also has a rather pleasant alcoholic kick. The perfect antidote to PMT. Of course, this choc fest can be served as a pudding, rather than a sweet snack, and men are welcome to dig in, too. Just let them dare say it's medicinal …

5 plain chocolate digestive biscuits
50g butter
100g plain chocolate (at least 72% cocoa solids)
150g Philadelphia cream cheese

100ml extra-thick double cream
100g icing sugar
7 tablespoons coffee-flavoured liqueur, such as Tia Maria

Put the biscuits in a plastic bag and bash them with a rolling pin until they are finely crushed. Melt the butter in a pan, add the biscuits and stir together. Put 50g of the chocolate in a bowl and either put it in the microwave for 2–3 minutes to melt, or else put the bowl over a pan of simmering water on the stove. Put the melted chocolate, cream cheese, double cream, icing sugar and the liqueur into a bowl and mix together until smooth. In a wine glass, layer 1 tablespoon of biscuit mixture followed by 1 tablespoon of the chocolate mixture, then repeat. Do the same in 2 more wine glasses. Take the rest of the chocolate and grate some of it over each pudding. If you have any self-restraint at all, chill for 1–2 hours, but if you are really so hormonal you feel you might be about to shoot someone, then maybe it's best if you scoff one straight away.

serves 3

Even the most confident cooks are scared of cooking for a crowd. I have to admit that there are actually a fair few Vicars' wives who would rather eat their own heads than entertain for 30. And, quite frankly, I used to feel the same way. All that chopping; all that standing at the stove; all those plates; all those knives and forks: why not just order pizzas? However, over time I've discovered there is something very lovely about feeding a big gang of people. In they all troop, shedding bags and coats and hats, and suddenly the house is alive and filled with warmth. I love to watch as they all sit round – on chairs, couches or even on the floor – feasting on plates of homely fare and laughing and talking. It feels almost tribal.

My first introduction to cooking for a crowd was in 1997. The Vicar had taken over the running of a teenage summer camp and, suddenly, when we had a Camp Reunion in frozen January, 40 leaders were coming for supper. The food had to be hot; it had to be tasty; and it had to be cheap. For me, it was, as is the phrase, a baptism by fire. I confess I was pretty daunted, but, on the night, seeing people relax and have a chance to catch up with each other after a day trawling round London in the freezing cold was in itself a pure delight. However, the fact they were doing so over plates of steaming grub I'd made myself was what really did it for me. Quite frankly, I felt like a deliriously happy Mother Hen who could barely keep herself from clucking.

It was this maternal pleasure that eradicated my fear of cooking for numbers. Yes, it is physically hard work; yes, it takes time, thought and organisation, but there's no magic about it. So, if someone like me, who is neither especially strong, nor particularly organised, can do it, I assure you so can you. And you might – honestly – even enjoy it …

Crowd Food

Summer gatherings

For me, summer get-togethers mean one thing: eating outside. Of course, the British summer being as it is, this luxury isn't always possible, and so there have been a fair few meals at our house that have had to be carted back indoors when the rain started to pour. However, it's always worth being optimistic and to at least plan to eat in the open air. Maybe because we do it so rarely, it inevitably feels so terribly special, and not only does everything taste better, but even the most melancholy of people seem happier, brighter; excited even.

My own memories of meals under sunny skies are invariably pleasant ones: a birthday barbecue in the garden of our old house followed by an impromptu game of rounders; a sit-down dinner of Spanish fare in our present home, a celebration on the terrace with baked asparagus and artichoke and lemon butter – all these meals conjure up feelings of joyful, and almost tearfully fond, nostalgia.

Barbecue for eight

If there is anything that proves the British have a fighting spirit, it is their loyalty to the barbecue. Despite the fact the sun often fails to shine; despite the fact the meat turns out either raw or burnt, we soldier on, and every year, come a hint of warmth, we enthusiastically ask friends round to crack open a beer and hover round the smoking coals.

The Australians, of course, are a dab hand at 'the Barbie'; for them it's second nature. In the hot summer of 2006, our Aussie former neighbours used to light up their barbecue every night as a matter of course, and there was not one sniff of carbon nor one instance of Salmonella. So what are the tricks to a successful barbecue that will actually produce food worth eating? I have to say that I never get involved in it: it's the one time the Vicar takes a turn at the stove. A logical, measured sort, he may not always produce perfectly cooked meat, but he certainly plans to.

Here are a few of his sensible tips to help you on your way:

'Light the barbecue at least an hour before you want to start cooking. I would do it before guests arrive, because once they are there it's easy to get involved in pouring drinks and chatting.

'Position the barbecue in a gentle draught not too near where people are standing, because it's not fun getting smoke in your eyes and Elisa will only start fretting about the state of her mascara. Place a table next to the barbecue on which to place the food to be cooked, your tongs, a water spray to banish any bursts of flame, and some oil and a brush to anoint both the grill and the meat (this prevents the meat from sticking).

'First arrange some firelighters in the bottom of the barbecue and then arrange the charcoal in a pyramid shape over the top, to a height of about 5cm or so. Light the firelighters and leave the fire to get going – it is ready when the coals are covered in whitish ash (in daylight), and at night you will see them glowing red, but there should be no flames. Spread out the charcoal, put on the grill and add more charcoal round the edges from time to time to keep the barbecue at a steady temperature.'

Thanks, Vicar. Now, may I make a suggestion? If you know the people who are coming reasonably well, why not ask them to bring something to throw on that barbecue? Perhaps enough to share with another person? Not only will this save you money and free you up to think about the accompaniments, it will also be a way of uniting the party. You could get the joys of people bellowing: 'Who wants one of my venison burgers?' or maybe there'll be jostlers for the Argentinian steak. At one barbecue at our house, my lovely, well-brought-up friend, Sarah K, arrived with swordfish. A physical fight nearly ensued and we all made do with two bites each.

For pudding post-barbecue, I suggest you play it simple. How about serving frozen berries with a white chocolate sauce? It is a doddle to make, but also indescribably irresistible.

STEAKS, FISH, OR WHATEVER OFFERINGS YOU ARE GIVEN

RED CABBAGE AND STILTON SLAW

A NICE PASTA SALAD (I PROMISE!)

GREEN SALAD

FROZEN BERRIES WITH WHITE CHOCOLATE SAUCE

serves 8

Red Cabbage and Stilton Slaw

When I made this for the very first time, my lovely neighbours did a taste test. And then they moved straight back to Australia. Thankfully, the slaw wasn't the issue, and neither was our neighbourly friendship. Nervous by disposition, I was on edge when we moved in here, as their roof terrace was right next to ours. What if they turned out to be axe-murderers? Thankfully, the only butchering they were interested in is what preceded their regular barbecues. It was they who suggested this salad would go well with a steak – barbecued, of course. Liz and Drew – this is for you.

Get out your food processor for this recipe. If you haven't got one, you could chop all this by hand. Disadvantage: it won't be so uniform; advantage: it will be good for your arm muscles (I'm not sure which ones).

1 small red cabbage, outer leaves
   and base removed
4 carrots, peeled
2 red onions, peeled
about 150g Stilton cheese

For the dressing:
12 tablespoons extra virgin olive oil
3 tablespoons red wine vinegar
4 teaspoons French mustard
2 garlic cloves, peeled and crushed
6 dessertspoons single cream

Fit the slicing attachment to your food processor and push the vegetables through it so it all looks grated up (or whichever of your attachments suits this best). Tip the contents out into a large serving bowl and crumble in the Stilton in tiny chunks. Whisk together all the dressing ingredients, pour it over the salad and toss to combine, then chill in the fridge until needed.

serves 8

A Nice Pasta Salad (I promise!)

Pasta salad is a strange beast: hot pasta needs very little lubricant to make it shine – just add a good bit of butter, some Parmesan and lots of salt and pepper and you are rewarded with a surprisingly good feast; cold pasta, on the other hand, is a very different matter. There are some who think it is just plain wrong to eat it this way and, having tasted my own fair share of damp, tasteless offerings at churchie get-togethers, I do sympathise with that sentiment. However, if pasta is dressed whilst it is still hot, and all worries about calories are thrown to one side, it is possible to make a pasta salad that sings.

This one may seem packed to the gills with ingredients, but they all blend together beautifully. Like the red cabbage slaw, it's a dish you'll have to force yourself to stop eating. When I served it at one particular summer get-together, I found one enthusiastic guest eating it for breakfast when I came down the next morning.

serves 8

1 red pepper, core removed

1 yellow or orange pepper, core
   removed

1 large courgette or 2 small, grated

6 spring onions, chopped

250g pasta (conchiglie is good, as
   the shell shapes fill with the tasty
   dressing)

150g feta cheese

120g Cheddar cheese

2 tablespoons basil leaves, shredded

1 tablespoon raisins (optional, but I
   think their little hit of sweetness

is rather pleasing)

1 tablespoon pine nuts, toasted
   until golden

For the dressing:

150ml olive oil

50ml white wine vinegar

2 teaspoons Dijon mustard

a pinch of sugar

5 tablespoons fresh pesto

salt and pepper

1–3 tablespoons good-quality
   mayonnaise (optional)

Put the kettle on and make yourself a nice cup of tea. Well, you can if you want, but actually, the boiling water is needed to cook the pasta in a bit. Preheat the grill to high, then halve the peppers and put them, skin-side up, underneath it. When the skins are black and charred, remove the peppers from the grill to cool. In a big salad bowl, throw in the grated courgette and the spring onions.

In a pan of boiling salted water, cook the pasta according to the instructions on the packet. Meanwhile, once the peppers have cooled, pull off their skins and snip the flesh into strips with kitchen scissors, and add them to the courgette and spring onions.

Now make the dressing: whisk together the oil, the vinegar, mustard, sugar and pesto, and season with salt and pepper. Once the pasta is cooked, drain it,

serves 8

A Nice Pasta Salad   265

return it to the pan and pour the dressing straight over. Add the pasta to the salad bowl, crumble in the feta and throw in the grated Cheddar and basil. Give everything a good stir and taste for seasoning.

At this point you can decide whether you want the pasta to be more unctuous still by stirring in some mayonnaise. I always do, and I've had no regrets. Add the raisins, if wished. Give it one last stir and, finally, scatter the toasted pine nuts over the top. Let the whole thing cool down, but I think it's nicer served not too icy cold.

Green Salad

For the salad:
1 little gem lettuce, chopped
80g watercress
¼ large cucumber, thinly sliced
2 handfuls of baby spinach

For the dressing:
3 tablespoons olive oil
1 tablespoon lemon juice
1 teaspoon Dijon mustard
salt and pepper

In a small bowl whisk together the ingredients for the dressing. Tip all the greenery into a large bowl and pour in enough dressing to coat each leaf in a lovely, glossy kiss.

serves 8

Frozen Berries with White Chocolate Sauce

How can something so easy taste so devilishly good?

600g white chocolate
600ml double cream
1kg frozen berries (bag of frozen
  ones is fine, if you take out any
  strawberries)

Break the chocolate into a heatproof bowl with the cream. Place it over a pan of barely simmering water and allow the chocolate to melt into the cream to make a smooth and silky sauce – this should take 20–30 minutes. About 5–10 minutes before you are ready to eat, take the berries out of the freezer and divide them among 8 plates. Transfer the sauce into a big jug and pour generously over each plate of fruit.

Spanish tapas for twelve

I love Spain. Every year, once winter has even half-promised to say its goodbyes, the Vicar and I head to our favourite Spanish city. I first stumbled on it as a student backpacker, fresh from a split with a boy. Its maze of higgledy-piggledy streets bewitched me. I stumbled around over the cobbles, delighted and entranced by men playing cards in the twilight, the sight of plant-filled courtyards and the sniff of garlic-scented dinners. And then I was lost. Thank goodness, then, that this place is a peninsula and the space between land and sea is somewhat sparse. Within two minutes I came upon the sea and a sunset – and music and flamenco dancing. Men stomped with more pride than the English could muster on a match day, and the women swirled against the backdrop of an orange sun, duly proud of hips and curves we Brits would long to cover in spandex.

As I watched I felt almost tearful: such a vivid, wonderful sight, and no one to share it with. Thankfully, the Vicar now loves this place, too, so every year we savour the sights and smells together and amble round little bars, grazing on tortillas and calamari and deliciously fresh prawns. The menu below is an attempt to capture some of that. Throw in some Rioja and some Spanish music, and you may even get people dancing. (Castanets optional.)

serves 12

My tortillas (see page 189 for recipe)

Platters of fresh anchovies, chorizo, olives, Serrano ham and Manchego cheese

Pan con tomate

Prawn and Serrano skewers

Pork Pinchitos

Mushrooms cooked in sherry

The fresh anchovies, meats and cheeses for the platters can be bought from a deli. Allow each person around 4 fresh anchovies, 4–5 chunks of chorizo, 3 slices of Serrano ham and a few pieces of Manchego. Buy good, juicy olives (not the slimy ones in a tin).

Pan Con Tomate

This is so utterly simple it seems impossible for it to taste so good. I was told about it years ago by Doctor S, who had just got back from a stay in Barcelona. I often make it to serve as an appetiser with drinks, especially if dinner is taking longer than I'd intended.

1 large, coarse, rustic loaf
2 garlic cloves, halved
8 ripe tomatoes, halved

extra virgin olive oil
salt

Cut the loaf into medium slices, then either toast them or bake them in the oven at 200°C/Gas Mark 6 for about 5 minutes until the bread is golden and crisp. Taking the cut side of the garlic, rub it over each slice of bread to release some of the garlic juice. Move on to a fresh garlic half when you have worked the best out of the old one. Next, take the tomatoes and rub those over the bread, squeezing out tomato juice as you go. If you wish, dice the tomato skins and sprinkle those on top. Finally, drizzle with the oil and, with a generous hand, grind over the salt. Eat as soon as possible.

serves 12

Prawn and Serrano Skewers

Tasty little numbers, these. This recipe makes enough for everyone to have 4 or 5 prawns each.

400g Serrano or Parma ham
48–60 large raw prawns, peeled
black pepper

2 tablespoons olive oil
3 lemons, cut into quarters, to serve

Soak 12-15 long wooden skewers in water for about 3 minutes before using – this will help them to stand the heat of the griddle. Cut the ham into slices big enough to wrap round the prawns. Each slice of ham should give you about 3 pieces. Wrap up your delicious seafood and, taking the skewers out of their water, slide on the prawns, making sure the ham is firmly fixed around them. Season generously and drizzle with the oil.

Heat a griddle pan until it is smoking hot and pop on the skewers. It should take 2–3 minutes per side for the prawns to cook and the ham to go crispy. Season with black pepper and serve immediately, offering the lemon wedges for squeezing over. Oh, and don't forget the napkins.

Pork Pinchitos

That's kebabs to you and me.

5 garlic cloves, peeled and finely
   chopped
2 teaspoons salt
3 teaspoons mild curry powder
1 teaspoon coriander seeds, crushed
2 teaspoons pimentón (smoked
   Spanish paprika – it comes either
   sweet or with more of a kick)

$^1/_2$ teaspoon dried thyme
black pepper
5 tablespoons olive oil
2 teaspoons dried oregano
2 tablespoons lemon juice
1kg cubed pork

In a mortar, crush the garlic with the salt using a pestle, then simply mix with all the other ingredients in a large bowl. Leave to marinate, covered, in the fridge for at least 2 hours. Meanwhile, soak 12 wooden skewers in water for about $^1/_2$ hour. Remove the skewers from the water just before you are ready to cook, and push the cubes of pork onto them (about 4 per skewer). Pop them on a baking tray and cook them under a hot grill – about 3 minutes should do it. Get them round the guests fast so they can eat them while they're good and hot.

makes 12 kebabs

Mushrooms Cooked in Sherry

Everyone has to partake of this nibble, otherwise there will be some present who reek of garlic, and others who don't; and that's just not fair.

175ml olive oil
1kg small chestnut or button
    mushrooms
20 garlic cloves, peeled and
    chopped

12 tablespoons dry sherry
juice of 2 lemons
1 teaspoon pimentón (see page 273)
salt and pepper
6 tablespoons parsley, chopped

Heat the oil in a large pan and sauté the mushrooms over high heat for about 2 minutes, stirring constantly. Lower the heat to medium and add all the remaining ingredients, bar the parsley. Cook for about 5 minutes or until the garlic and mushrooms have softened. Remove from the heat, sprinkle with chopped parsley and serve with lots of white bread for dunking.

A midsummer banquet for eight

A rare thing: a blistering day in the heart of summer. That's worth a celebration in itself. The fact that it was also the Vicar's birthday doubled the need for a large dose of merriment and jubilation. I'd laid the table in the garden with good china and bowls of headily-scented white roses and it looked, if I say so myself, the epitome of the particular beauty of an English summer. The Vicar had even mown the lawn. We drifted through the meal, made dreamy by afternoon wine, revelling in the meal's fresh, light flavours and the company of good friends. It was one of those days you never want to end.

MARGARITAS

ROASTED RED PEPPER GAZPACHO

LOBSTER, KING PRAWN AND MANGO SALAD WITH LIME AND CORIANDER

RICH CHOCOLATE MOUSSE TORTE

serves 8

Margaritas

Per glass:
40ml fresh lime juice (about 2 limes)
50ml tequila

1 tablespoon orange Curaçao
ice cubes, for mixing, or crushed ice,
to serve

This is easiest made in a cocktail shaker, so make one drink at a time. Measure out and mix together the lime juice, tequila, and the orange Curaçao. Shake with ice or pour it over crushed ice. Before pouring out the drink, feel free to tip the damp rim of the glass into salt for a fancy effect. Then repeat the process for the rest of your thirsty friends.

For a really summery take on this drink, mix in a little puréed strawberry. Yum.

serves 8

Roasted Red Pepper Gazpacho

I don't really go for cold soups, but this one is an exception to my own personal rule. Punchy, yet refreshing, it is bursting with Mediterranean flavours. It's also a sight to behold.

This recipe makes enough for twelve people, which gives you the option for seconds, or to have leftovers for another sunny day.

4 large red peppers
1.8kg ripe, vine-ripened tomatoes
2 cucumbers
1 ciabatta loaf
8 tablespoons sherry vinegar
2 garlic cloves, peeled and crushed
300ml olive oil
2 teaspoons caster sugar
Maldon salt and white pepper

For the garnishes:
2 tablespoons extra virgin olive oil, plus extra to serve
4 vine-ripened tomatoes, skinned, seeded and cut into small dice
½ cucumber, peeled, seeded and cut into small dice
8 spring onions, trimmed and thinly sliced
4 hardboiled eggs, peeled and cut into small dice
about 24 ice cubes, to serve

Preheat the oven to 220°C/Gas Mark 7. Roast the red peppers, whole, for about 25 minutes, turning now and then, until the skins are quite black.

Meanwhile, skin the tomatoes by popping them in a bowl filled with just-boiled water for few minutes, then remove them from the water carefully and peel away the skin. Cut each tomato into quarters and scoop out the seeds into a sieve set over a small bowl. Roughly chop the flesh and press the juices from the seed pulp through the sieve. Peel the cucumbers using a vegetable peeler or a sharp knife, cut them in half lengthways, scoop out the seeds with a teaspoon and roughly chop the flesh. Cut 4 thin slices from the ciabatta and set aside for the garnish. Remove the crusts from the remainder of the loaf and whizz into breadcrumbs in a food processor. You need about 100g in total.

Remove the roasted red peppers from the oven and leave them to cool. Once cool enough to handle, break them open, peel off the black and blistered skin with your fingers and pull out and discard the stalks and seeds. Roughly chop the flesh and turn the oven down to 200°C/Gas Mark 6.

In a liquidiser or food processor, blend the red peppers, the tomato flesh and strained juice, the cucumbers and the breadcrumbs with all the other soup ingredients. Whizz together until smooth, tasting for seasoning. (You will probably have to do this in quite a few batches, depending on the size of your liquidiser.) Pour the blended mixture into a large bowl and thin the soup to the required consistency using cold water. I'm afraid it is difficult to give an exact amount of water needed to thin down the soup, as this will very much depend on the water content of your tomatoes and cucumber. So, add it gradually and use just enough for it to lose that porridge-like look, but so that it's not too watery – you might need anything up to 600ml. Cover and chill for at least 2 hours or until very, very cold.

For the croûtons, tear the 4 reserved slices of bread into small, rough pieces and, in a small bowl, toss them with the 2 tablespoons of oil until well coated. Spread the pieces over a baking tray and bake in the oven for 4–5 minutes or until crisp and lightly golden. Remove and leave to cool.

To serve, put all the garnishes into separate small bowls, except the ice cubes. Ladle the soup into chilled bowls, drizzle with a little olive oil and add a couple of ice cubes to each. Leave everyone to garnish their own soup with whatever they like, as it is quite fun to 'prettify' your own food.

Lobster, King Prawn and Mango Salad with Lime and Coriander

This is treat food of the highest order. It is highly unlikely to happen, but if the Queen popped round one day, I'd be happy to serve this up. On my best china, of course. I'm sure Her Majesty would approve.

3 x 750g cooked lobsters (1 x 750g lobster will yield approx. 275g meat)

150g sugar snap peas

800g Jersey Royal potatoes, to serve

400g cooked tiger prawns, peeled

2 medium mangoes, peeled and thickly sliced

1 bunch spring onions, trimmed and thinly sliced

3 tablespoons coriander leaves, roughly torn

1 red chilli, de-seeded and finely chopped

salt and pepper

For the lime dressing:

4 tablespoons light olive oil

3 tablespoons fresh lime juice (about 3 limes)

salt and pepper

Cracking lobsters can seem daunting, but it's fine, I promise. First, twist off the claws and legs (the latter can be discarded), then break the claws into pieces at the joints. Crack the shell with the back of a knife or a heavy rolling pin. Once you are in, remove the yukky grey roe and the weird hard tentacle that runs head to tail. Then, try to remove the meat in as large pieces as possible. Cut the lobster in half lengthways; lift the meat out of the tail and slice it across into thin slices. Put the slices into a bowl and allow it to come back to room temperature about 30 minutes before you want to serve it. For the dressing, simply whisk the ingredients together in a bowl with $1/4$ teaspoon of salt and a little pepper.

Meanwhile, drop the sugar snap peas into a pan of boiling salted water, bring back to the boil until cooked, drain and refresh under running cold water. Drain well and set them aside. Shortly before you want to serve the salad, put the new potatoes into a pan of well-salted water, bring to the boil and simmer for about 15 minutes or until just tender.

Whisk the dressing briefly and toss 3 tablespoons of it with the lobster. Set it aside to lightly marinate.

Place the prawns and mango in a large, shallow salad bowl, add the sugar snap peas, spring onions, coriander, chilli, salt and pepper and the rest of the dressing, and toss together. Add the lobster at the end, and toss gently once more. Serve straight away with the hot potatoes in a separate bowl.

Rich Chocolate Mousse Torte

The perfect finale to this summer spectacular. After two light courses, it's only right to indulge in something rather richer: and, of course, it has to be chocolate. This torte serves eight to ten people, so it might leave you a slice or two for another day – if you're lucky!

This dessert needs to be made ahead, which means you can bask in the sunshine at the banqueting table and enjoy your day.

For the biscuit case:
50g plain chocolate (at least 60% cocoa solids)
2 tablespoons cocoa powder
50g butter
175g digestive biscuits
2 tablespoons golden caster sugar

For the filling:
1 teaspoon instant coffee granules
150g plain chocolate (at least 60% cocoa solids)
3 large fresh eggs
1 large egg yolk
1 teaspoon vanilla extract
4 tablespoons brandy or rum
3 tablespoons golden caster sugar

For the topping:
450ml double cream
1 tablespoon caster sugar
1 teaspoon cocoa powder

Remove the base from a 20cm clip-sided tin and lightly butter the ring. Place it directly onto a flat serving plate, upside-down, holding it in place on each side with a small piece of Blue Tac. Line the sides with a strip of non-stick baking paper.

For the biscuit case, break the chocolate into a heatproof bowl and add the cocoa powder and butter. Place it over a pan of barely simmering water, but not touching the water, and leave until melted, then stir until smooth. Put the digestive biscuits and the sugar into a food processor and blitz until you get fine crumbs. Stir them into the melted chocolate mixture, then tip them into the lined ring and, using the back of a dessertspoon, press the crumbs firmly onto the base and at least 4cm up the sides in a thick, even layer. Chill in the fridge while you make the filling.

Dissolve the coffee in 4 tablespoons of boiling water. Put the coffee and the chocolate into a large heatproof bowl, pop it over a pan of hot water (as above) until it is glossy and melted, then stir until smooth. Separate the eggs into two bowls. Add the 1 egg yolk to the bowl with the other yolks, then add the vanilla extract and mix together well. Stir into the chocolate and coffee mixture thoroughly and then stir in the brandy or rum.

Whisk the egg whites in a bowl until they are just beginning to show signs of stiffening, then gradually whisk in the sugar to form a floppy meringue. Gently fold it into the chocolate mixture, then pour the whole thing into the biscuit crumb case and chill for at least 4 hours, or overnight, until firm.

To serve, carefully remove the sides of the tin and peel away the paper. Softly whip the cream with the sugar until only just stiff, then spoon over the top of the torte and swirl with the back of the spoon. Dust with the cocoa powder and serve, cut into wedges. A bowl of strawberries on the side would be nice.

Cooking for crowds

Okay, cooking for a big gang does make you feel a bit queasy, and, I won't lie to you, it does take a little thought and effort, and costs a fair bit, too. These days, especially if you want meat or fish in the mix, cooking for under £3 a head is hard to pull off – unless the butcher or fishmonger is the person lying next to you at night. Here, unnatural to me though it is, I've put my sensible head on and I'm going to offer you a few tried-and-tested tips as to how to keep the panic levels down. The Vicar will be proud of me ...

Plan ahead

When it comes to food and eating, most people like to have a choice. I know cooking more than one thing feels like it doubles the burden, but in some ways it does actually make the cooking preparation less boring and the quantities (and the stirring of them) more manageable. If I am cooking for 40 people, I'd do something for 20–25 in one of my cauldrons and make it the day before so I can reheat it on the day. I would also, on the day itself, make something for the same number that can be cooked in the oven. It's also a good idea to offer a meat-free alternative for about six to eight people (even non-vegetarians can be tempted to shun the farmyard at times). However, if this all feels too ambitious, go for one big dish: no-one has ever knocked a well-made lasagne, or a creamy macaroni cheese jazzed up with wholegrain mustard, leeks, or cherry tomatoes.

Phone a friend

You might feel you need someone you trust to give you a hand, maybe even to help you cook. To be honest, I love cooking alone. I am a crazily up and down little soul and the calm solidity that cooking brings is something that I need. (And something my kind and quiet Vicar is grateful for, having the loopy wife that he does.) However, I do need a trusted friend when it comes to serving it all up. Getting a hot dinner out to a big crowd when you aren't used to it is quite something; you have to be utterly charming and briskly efficient at the same time. So, do yourself a favour and get yourself an extra pair of hands. Phone a friend. NOW!

Equipment

If you are cooking a dish for 20 people on the top of the stove, you do need the vast cauldron-type-thing that I have constantly raved about through this book. If you are serving rice or pasta, you will need two. I am a big fan of preparing couscous for big groups, because as it only needs boiling water poured over it, you can make it in the bowl you intend to serve it in. Or just buy lots of good bread and offer that as the starch-provider. Baked potatoes are also easy, but remember that the more stuff you put in the oven, the more time things will take to cook.

If you are cooking something, or things, in the oven, you need a big baking tray or roasting tin – or use two if you have to. I know serving things from a big metal dish isn't exactly elegant, but people will forgive you once they have tasted the contents.

Count up your cutlery, plates and glasses. If you haven't enough, introduce yourself to your neighbours and beg for ones they don't treasure, or go to Ikea and stock up on cheapies. If you are buying wine for your meal, many places offer free glass hire or, again, borrow or buy inexpensive stuff.

Food and drinks

Plan the menu at least a week in advance, if possible. Find out numbers and ask your guests if they don't like red meat or are vegetarians. If you want to keep costs down but want to serve meat, go for recipes that require cheaper cuts or use mince, which can be bulked up with a tasty sauce. If you are making more than one dish – something with red meat, something with chicken or fish, and maybe a veggie option, too – try to make sure that the accompaniments go with each main.

Write out a detailed shopping list and check it for quantities. If you are serving salad, remember that in the old days bags of salad didn't exist, and also that whole lettuces stretch further and are cheaper. Remember to include olive oil on your list, and bear in mind that you might be using it both for cooking and for dressing salads. Don't forget the napkins and a tablecloth – if you are happy with using a disposable table cover and paper napkins, write them down on your list of things to buy.

If you know the people who are coming well and it is to be a relaxed affair, don't feel embarrassed about asking a few people to bring a pudding. Tell them how many you need it to feed and assure them they can feel free to buy if they don't like cooking (or just ask for puds from those guests who do). As for wine, I wouldn't dare assume I know how much (or little) your friends drink. The average bottle serves six small glasses (although these days most places seem to serve wine in large vats). Remember that some people will be driving or just not drinking, so make sure you also provide juice and water – both still and sparkling. (I don't think I could live without sparkling water, I positively twitch with panic if I have none in the house.)

If you are ordering the food online, arrange for it to arrive two days before the event. Then, if there is something missing you have time to get it. As you will be delivered a vast quantity of produce, plan to have an empty fridge for when it arrives: no stocking up beforehand – live on beans on toast for a few days if you have to. If you are shopping for the food yourself, I would still go two days before. As efficient as I am sure you are, it is still possible to forget something. Bread is the only thing you want to run out for on the big day – or send that nice friend of yours to get it.

The day before

Make anything that can be happily (and safely) reheated on the day. This especially applies to any meat braises or stews, which benefit from being given time to settle down and for the ingredients to relax together. Incidentally, cutting up meat for stews for groups can take an awfully long time, and doing it is very, very dull. So, if you are buying the meat from a butcher, ask them to do it for you; that's what they are there for.

Other jobs to do the day before include: making the salad dressing, if you are serving salad; gathering together plates, cutlery and glasses; tidying and cleaning the house and making sure there is clear space somewhere for people to dump their coats, bags and other stuff.

On the big day

Prepare any main course that will need to be made fresh up to the point that it goes in the oven. Start this in the morning, as cooking in bulk will take more time than your usual meals. When that is done, prepare your house. Arrange chairs for people to perch on, scatter cushions around the floor and decide on lighting (if it's an evening event). Provide side tables on which people can abandon stray plates and glasses, and think about music, mentally noting to get someone to play DJ once the 'do' kicks off.

Get your serving area ready. You will need a big table with enough space to serve your lovely food; mats on which to put your cauldron, baking dish, or whatever; serving spoons; and space to stand behind the table to serve up. You could let people serve themselves, but people can get too dithery/greedy this way and you (and the trusted friend) can move them on and get everyone sorted before those who are still hungry can come back to help themselves to seconds. I generally put the stack of dinner plates (with napkins interlaced between them) on the corner of the first table that people encounter, or else on a small table just before the one at which I am serving.

It's a good idea to put the drinks and glasses somewhere else away from the food serving area. When people arrive, encourage someone who is shy and loves being given a job to pour people a drink or else beckon people to help themselves. If you are serving nibbles, don't put them on this table or else you will end up with many gutsy friends standing around and chowing down, making it harder for others to get a drink. Instead, scatter them (I mean in bowls, not like rose petals at a wedding) around the house. Whew, that's the sensible bit over. Let's get back to the fun stuff.

Winter Feasts

Despite the fact that I obsessively love sunshine and the crisp delights of summer food, I embrace the change in our seasons. Yes, I detest feeling cold and am pretty miserable when the house begs for warmth and the joy of central heating (apparently, I have to wait until November before it's turned on). However, the fact that our soil and animals produce exactly what someone in need of bone-warming succour wants to eat is something that never ceases to amaze me. It helps me cope with icy radiators no end. The vegetables are earthy and full of comfort, and cheap cuts of flavoursome meat lend themselves to heady stews that fill the house with the soothing smell of contented warmth.

All this means that entertaining in the winter is really rather wonderful. Fires can flicker; the candles can be lit, endowing even the grimiest of homes with a dreamy feel. On the stove, or in your oven, will be something which will entice your guests into the kitchen, plates at the ready. Winter food – utterly consoling, gentle and comforting – is the perfect medicine for the bite of a chilly day. Adding to its appeal is the fact that it is cheap, too. Price check a plate of lamb stew next to a summery dish of salmon and asparagus and you have enough money left over to invite more friends over than you ever thought …

A winter dinner for twenty

Some friends asked to borrow our lounge for a meeting. It suited us fine, as we were going out and it meant we had twenty free babysitters. Shame we couldn't have spread them out over twenty evenings of nights out on the town, but you can't have everything. As the twenty people concerned were journeying from all over the place to camp at ours for the evening, I thought I'd cook something for tired travellers: my richly exotic Bedouin lamb followed by honey-heavy baked plums. Food fit for nomads.

BEDOUIN LAMB

HONEYED PLUMS

Bedouin Lamb

This dish is heady and mysterious and has a huge depth of flavour, while the dates lend a delicate touch of sweetness. Ideally, you should prepare it in advance and reheat it gently on the day you want to eat it.

When I first made this dish, in the first week of January 2003, that's exactly what I did. We had a massive crowd coming for dinner the next day, so I cooked the night before the party. However, as I'd only had my daughter on Christmas Eve, I asked the Vicar if he minded if I took myself to bed early (as I knew I'd be up in the middle of the night feeding our new, hungry little scrap), and could he please turn the lamb off later and cover and leave it to cool? It was around 4 in the morning, and feeding time well behind me, when I woke again, roused by a very strong smell emanating from the kitchen. I ran down to find the pan still on the stove and the lamb was all gone, thick carbon having taken its place. I was found sobbing bitterly on the stairs outside the kitchen some time later by the (very apologetic) perpetrator of the crime. Needless to say, the flowers he bought me the next day were a particularly large bunch …

serves 20

4.5kg leg or shoulder of lamb, cut
    into 2cm cubes
seasoned flour
20 tablespoons olive oil
5 onions, peeled and sliced
10 garlic cloves, peeled and crushed
30 cloves
3 teaspoons fresh ginger (or use
    'Lazy Ginger' from a jar), grated

6 teaspoons ground cinnamon
3 teaspoons ground coriander
2 litres lamb stock (fresh, or use a
    good-quality liquid bouillon)
1 bottle red wine
250g stoned dates
large bunch of coriander, chopped
2 x 400g tins of chickpeas
salt and pepper

The most time-consuming part of preparing this dish is cutting up the lamb, so if you have bought the meat from your butcher you will save yourself a lot of bother if you ask him, or her for that matter, to do the job for you. If you can face the task of doing it yourself, do feel free to have those kitchen scissors on hand to help. I know I have constantly mentioned how useful they are, but many people don't have great knives, or even if they do, they aren't sharp enough, and not all of us have knife skills that are exactly speed-of-light. So, swallow your pride and wield those scissors.

Once the lamb is in chunks, toss it in the seasoned flour and heat 5 tablespoons of the oil in a very large pan (I used my cauldron). Brown the lamb in batches, restraining yourself from overcrowding the pan. Add more oil in between each batch – another 5 tablespoons or so – and remove the browned lamb to a large dish or roasting tin. Pour the rest of the oil into the pan, add the onions and garlic and fry until soft. Now throw in all the spices and stir them round for 1 minute or so, then chuck all the lamb back into the pan. Add the stock, the wine, the dates, and 1 tablespoon of the chopped coriander. Bring everything to the boil, turn the heat down and simmer for about 2–2½ hours, or until the lamb is tender. Add the chickpeas 20 minutes before the end of the cooking time.

If you haven't got a massive pan, just brown the lamb in batches in the biggest one you've got, then remove the meat to a really big roasting tin. Fry the onions and garlic in the pan, add the spices, the stock, the red wine and the dates, and bring to the boil. Then put the roasting tin on the top of the stove, add the mixture from the pan and all the rest of the ingredients, and bring it back to the boil. Finally, pop the tin in an oven preheated to 150°C/Gas Mark 2 for around 2½ hours. Add the chickpeas 20 minutes before the end of the cooking time.

Season the dish with salt and pepper and either sprinkle the rest of the coriander into the pan or tin and stir it in gently, or scatter it on top of each individual portion when served up onto plates. Eat with couscous and a big green salad.

serves 20

Bedouin Lamb   293

Honeyed Plums

This recipe is effortless, and it's a good way of using plums and bringing out their beauty. Served with Greek yogurt, they make a light, yet satisfying, end to this warm winter feast.

40 plums, halved and the stones removed
2 cinnamon sticks, snapped in half

250ml red wine
8 tablespoons runny honey

Simply put the plums in 1 or 2 roasting tins or a shallow baking dish and arrange the pieces of cinnamon sticks amongst them. Splash over the red wine evenly, then drizzle over the honey so that each plum gets a little anointing. The plums need to be cooked for around 30–40 minutes at 190°C/Gas Mark 5. Check on them every now and then and add a splash of water if they begin to dry out and stick to the dish. I think they are best served warm, not hot, so wait for them to cool a little before serving. Offer them with some good-quality vanilla ice cream.

Curry for a crowd

A friend had bravely offered to cook for 'special diets' on a children's camp and found herself faced with, among other challlenges, a gluten-free vegetarian and a limited range of storecupboard ingredients. This was her solution to the problem.

CHEAP AND CHEERY CHICKPEA CURRY

CUCUMBER RAITA

MANGO KULFI

serves 30–35

Cheap and Cheery Chickpea Curry

This is adapted from a recipe my friend found on www.veganfamily.co.uk. It's cheap as chips (even cheaper if you pop to a cash-and-carry, or the like, and get catering-size tins), but tastier and better for you.

7 onions, peeled and very finely chopped

100ml olive oil

20 garlic cloves, peeled and crushed

7 tablespoons curry powder

7 apples, peeled and finely chopped

1 x 2.5kg tin tomatoes

7 peppers (feel free to use a mixture of colours), cores removed and finely chopped

1 bag raisins (approx. 500g)

1 small bag desiccated coconut (approx. 250g)

2 x 2.5kg tins chickpeas, drained and rinsed

1kg frozen peas

salt and pepper

600g young leaf spinach

This recipe requires 7 chopped onions, so I'd recommend getting your food processor out and putting in its chopping attachment. Heat the oil in a very large pan (yes, you guessed it, my cauldron is out again), and fry the onions and garlic for around 10 minutes on a low heat to soften. Add the curry powder and apples and stir for 1–2 minutes. After that, slop in the tomatoes and add the peppers, raisins and coconut. Cook for approximately 15 minutes, then pour in the chickpeas and cook for a further 10 minutes (stir it all diligently and keep the heat low, or it will stick to the bottom). Add the peas and cook for a further 5 minutes, before seasoning to taste. Shortly before serving, add the spinach and cook until it wilts. Serve with basmati rice (you will need about 1kg for this number of people), about 15 big naan breads (which can be torn up and shared amongst them), and a selection of chutneys, such as lime pickle or mango chutney.

Cucumber Raita

1 small cucumber (approx 400g)
1.2 litres Greek yogurt
4 garlic cloves, peeled and crushed
salt and pepper

a few big handfuls of fresh mint
leaves, shredded
cumin seeds, to serve

Finely grate the cucumber into a colander lined with kitchen towel, which will help to drain off some of the water. When drained, tip the grated cucumber into a large bowl and mix with the rest of the ingredients (except the cumin seeds). Leave to chill in the fridge, then scatter with cumin seeds just before serving.

serves 30–35

Mango Kulfi

Until recently, I'd always assumed kulfi was a drink: I must have been confusing it with lassi. Kulfi is an Indian-style ice cream, a perfect dessert to follow the chickpea curry. Real kulfi is made with milk and is simmered for an age until it takes on a deliciously rich and creamy consistency. Here the cooking time is speeded up by using what my mother calls 'evap' instead of normal milk.

6 tablespoons cornflour	**6 ripe mangoes**
3.6 litres evaporated milk	**1 teaspoon ground cardamom**
150g caster sugar	**900ml single cream**

Blend the cornflour with 6 tablespoons of cold water and set aside. In your large pan, quickly bring the evaporated milk to the boil then add the cornflour mixture and simmer for 2 minutes or until it is the consistency of pouring custard. Stir in the sugar over the heat until it has all dissolved, then pour the mixture into a big bowl, or a couple of bowls, and leave it to cool.

Peel the mangoes and slice the fruit around the stone into the bowl of a food processor, then blend it to a smooth purée. Stir this sticky purée into the cooled custard mix, add the cardamom and cream and then press the whole lot through a sieve into a clean bowl. At this point, you can either churn the mixture in an ice cream maker or, if you don't have an ice cream maker, do the job by hand. Pour the mixture into a few large plastic containers and cover with lids, then freeze until firm, but not rock solid – a few hours should do it. After this time, remove the containers, transfer the contents to a food processor and blend until smooth, then return to the containers and freeze for another hour or so. Repeat this process twice more until you get the right consistency. Spoon the kulfi into 36 tall, freezer-proof moulds (washed-out small yogurt pots are ideal). Freeze for at least 8 hours or until firm and hand them to your guests to eat with teaspoons.

Alternatively, if you want an easier life, serve the melon with ginger as described on page 209 as the dessert. Or you could even buy in some lemon sorbet and drizzle it with the Italian liqueur, limoncello. To keep things even cheaper and delightfully cheery, why not hand out ice cream cones, complete with their very own chocolate flake?

serves 36

Mango Kulfi   299

New Year's Day brunch for thirty

I think New Year's Day is one of my favourite days of the year. I know it's silly, but somehow I always feel that the slate has been wiped clean and there's a sense of anticipation and curiosity about the year to come. Traditionally, we Beynons celebrate by holding an all-day party. I don't really like the night before, as there is so much pressure to have a fabulously magical time that it is often hopelessly disappointing.

However, the first day of the year holds no such expectations. People are usually tired, but keen to cling on to the holidays and evade the grim reality of the hard graft to come. All this makes it the perfect day to have friends over for soothing sustenance, delicious drinks and perhaps some quiet music or an old film. This brunch is ideal for a crowd because you can prepare the bubble and squeak and the rich tomato sauce the day before, and then on the day put the sausages in a low oven and just cook everything else to order. Or get someone else to do it for you, as I did.

SAUSAGES

POACHED EGGS

BUBBLE AND SQUEAK PATTIES

RICH TOMATO SAUCE WITH HARISSA

serves 30

I don't think I need to explain to you how to cook sausages or poach eggs, so all I will say is that you should try to buy good, meaty sausages. You should allow 30–40 minutes for them to cook in a low oven at 150°C/Gas Mark 2. The poached eggs should take 5 minutes when cooked in one of those poaching pans. Do them in batches of however many your pan will hold. Everyone seemed happy enough with one of everything – although some people did have seconds, too.

Bubble and Squeak Patties

5kg floury maincrop potatoes, such as King Edwards or Maris Piper
2 green cabbages
350g butter

1.2kg smoked bacon lardons or smoked streaky bacon, chopped
1 x 284ml tub double cream
salt and pepper

Peel the potatoes (preferably with a friend, as 5kg is an awful lot of potatoes; the Vicar nobly got stuck in with me) and cut them into medium-sized chunks. Put them in a huge pan, or a few pans if you don't have one big enough, of boiling, liberally salted water and cook for about 20–25 minutes or until soft. Meanwhile, shred the cabbages and fry in batches, using around 50g of butter at a time, until the cabbage has softened and browned slightly. In another pan, fry the bacon pieces until cooked but not crispy (you don't need to use any oil) and heat through the cream and the rest of the butter in another pan.

When they are ready, drain the potatoes well in a colander, wait until the steam dies down and then return them to the pan and mash them thoroughly. Add the rest of the ingredients, not forgetting the seasoning. Chill in the fridge for an hour or two, or overnight if you're making this in advance. When you are ready to cook, form the bubble and squeak mixture into patties, either using a cake cutter or a ramekin. Fry to order in about a tablespoon of olive oil: they will take around 7–10 minutes to cook and should be flipped over halfway through.

Rich Tomato Sauce with Harissa

If you have any of this sauce left over, please don't fret; it is lovely with pasta or you can thin it out with water and eat it as a soup.

3 tablespoons olive oil
8 onions, peeled and finely sliced
2 garlic cloves, peeled and crushed
6 x 400g tins chopped tomatoes

1 generous teaspoon harissa paste
  (more if you are brave)
salt and pepper

Heat the oil in a pan and fry the onions and garlic until softened, then chuck in the tomatoes. Let it all bubble away and reduce a bit before adding the harissa and some seasoning, to taste. Serve a couple of tablespoons per person, alongside the bubble and squeak patties.

serves 30

Funeral Fare

Let's face it, food and funerals are not easy bedfellows. Death tends to put you off a slap-up dinner even more than a trip to the dentist; and yet, because people may have travelled from afar, it is only right that you offer them something to keep their strength up or to just hold their hunger-driven hysteria at bay. Not only that but, if the funeral is of a loved-one, preparing the food gives you something useful to do.

I can vividly remember how, at my father's do, my mother and sister went into a sandwich-making frenzy. I kid you not, by the time they'd finished there was no bread left anywhere in Pembrokeshire. The whole occasion was, if I'm honest, somewhat surreal. The Vicar, a mere boyfriend at the time, had come home with me in loving support. Unfortunately, it was all very last-minute and he had nothing to wear for the big day. At the time, it didn't strike my mother or me as particularly strange to dress him in my dead father's clothes, but thinking back, we can now both see that it was wrong. Especially because, despite my mother's assurances that he looked really rather nice, they did not fit him awfully well, what with the sleeves being halfway up his arms, and all. Then there was the memorable burial. Standing on a Welsh hill in a howling gale, my tiny little mother moved forward to peek at Father's descending coffin – a touching scene – except for the fact that the wind picked up exactly at that moment and she had to be snatched from joining her husband in an early grave.

This little lot here makes enough for fifty guests, with each person allocated 1 sandwich (that's 2 slices of bread). At our church, we have often had sandwiches inside the church for everyone, before closer friends and family head off for a smaller gathering elsewhere. If it is to be an intimate do, just halve everything, or whatever, and if making a truckload of sandwiches feels all too much, there's always the option of buying in.

The quantities listed below should make 12 each of egg mayonnaise and cress; Cheddar and mango chutney; chicken mayonnaise and bacon, and 14 of the ham with Dijon mustard. Believe me, if you ever have to prepare this little lot you may never want to look at a sandwich again.

Please don't think me condescending to be telling you how to make a simple, unfancy sandwich; it's just that quantities like this can be rather overwhelming and there are times in life when we actually want to be bossed about and told exactly what to do. The funeral of a loved-one can be one of them. However, I will leave it up to you to decide if you want to remove the crusts: it would certainly feed a lot of birds!

To make this many sandwiches you will need 3 loaves of brown bread and 3 of white – buy it sliced to make life a little easier.

EGGS AND CRESS SANDWICHES

CHEDDAR AND MANGO CHUTNEY SANDWICHES

CHICKEN, MAYONNAISE AND BACON SANDWICHES

HAM WITH DIJON MUSTARD SANDWICHES

serves 50

Egg and Cress Sandwiches

12 large eggs

250ml good-quality mayonnaise

salt and pepper

2 punnets of cress

Make sure the eggs are at room temperature and not coming straight from the fridge, then divide them between 2 big pans. (It's important not to crowd the pans so that all the eggs will cook properly.) Cover the eggs with cold water and turn on the heat to high. When the water reaches boiling point, turn down the heat and cook for 7 minutes. Once the time is up, remove the eggs and plunge them straight into cold water.

Peel them (a job I loathe, so, funeral it might be, but I'd have some jolly music on to keep me from going mad), then roughly slice them before mashing them with the mayonnaise. Season with salt and pepper and gently stir in the cress. Spread this mixture between 24 slices of brown bread to make 12 sarnies. Cut into triangles and cover, chilling until needed.

Cheddar and Mango Chutney Sandwiches

290g butter   **75g salad leaves**
150ml good-quality mango chutney   **400g Cheddar cheese**

It's up to you as to whether you want to slice or grate the cheese here; but if you go for the slicing option, the cheese needs to be even, so I'd play safe and go for grating. Butter 24 pieces of brown bread and spread over a little mango chutney and a layer of salad leaves. Sprinkle over the cheese, but don't do as I do and overstuff – you will only end up with grated cheese on your carpet. Put the other slices of bread on top, cut into triangles and cover, chilling until needed.

Chicken, Mayonnaise and Bacon Sandwiches

7 chicken breasts
salt and pepper

14 rashers of smoked streaky bacon
250ml good-quality mayonnaise

Preheat the oven to 180°C/Gas Mark 4. Place the chicken breasts in a large, oiled roasting tin and season with salt and pepper. Cook them in the oven and check them after 30 minutes: they are ready when the meat feels firm to the touch and the juices run clear when pierced with a knife. Whilst they are cooking, grill the bacon in batches until fairly crisp. Allow both the bacon and the chicken to cool, then snip the bacon into thin slices using kitchen scissors and cut the chicken into small, bite-sized chunks.

Mix them together with the mayonnaise, season and divide the mixture between 24 slices of white bread to make another 12 sandwiches. Cut into triangles and cover, chilling until needed.

Ham with Dijon Mustard Sandwiches

335g butter
¹/₃ x 180g jar of Dijon mustard

85g salad leaves
14 slices of good ham

An easier one, this. Butter the rest of the white bread and smear 14 slices with a smidgen of the mustard. Scatter over some salad leaves, lay over a slice of ham per sandwich and slap the other piece of bread on top. Whew, done. Cut into triangles and cover, chilling until needed.

Little bites

The jury's out on canapés; they are so pretty, but they are also in danger of looking prissy and never, ever filling you up. There are many who would hurl those smoked-salmon mini bagels and their brie and cranberry parcel friends out of the window and head straight for a good, solid, sit-down dinner. However, I think canapés do have their place. At the wedding where the photographs are taking just too long and you are loitering around on the grass, running out of things to say, the arrival of a plate of frivolous little mouthfuls perks everyone up. Suddenly everyone is, 'Oooh, have you had that one?' 'Mmmm, that one's really nice.' If the Vicar's at the bash, he does have a tendency to go a bit canapé crazy, behaving as though each proffered mouthful could be his last. He either insists on moving position so he can pounce on the poor waitress as soon as she enters the room, or he engages the young thing in light-hearted and charming conversation whilst hoovering his way through the plate. He even ropes me into his filthy practice, nodding meaningfully at his favourite morsels so he can partake of my booty as well as his own. What a delicious villain!

While being served pretty little mouthfuls at a wedding is one thing, making them yourself is quite another. Surely no one in this day and age, when it's hard enough to get dinner on the table, would bother with all that fiddling about? They'd have to be out of their minds …

Well, I admit it: I am, for I do make canapés. I make them because they are fun and a talking point and they bring people together. I make them because, whilst I am a London girl who laps up the cocktail of experience that going out in the capital offers, I sometimes want to re-create a sense of opulent, festive glamour in my own home. And canapés can provide that: those delicate little bites exude the very essence of decadence and elegant celebration.

The antithesis of hearty fare, they also provide men with the challenge of demolishing as many as possible, and weight-conscious women the chance to fool themselves into thinking that something so small is virtually calorie-free.

It does have to be said, though, that these heavenly little eats that disappear in a moment, can take a devilishly long time to assemble. Professional party caterers suggest providing 12–16 canapés per person for a full, proper feed-up. To prepare that number for twenty people is definitely a whole day's work, without factoring in the shopping for ingredients. I once did a drinks party and allowed for 9 canapés a head, however, I did also provide a big deli platter of good bread, cheeses, olives and hams. Not quite as elegant, maybe, but it stopped people leaving early and gave them something to soak up the cocktails.

Canapés for twenty

You will need in the region of 200 canapés to serve twenty guests, more if you can face the work. Plan to offer a mixture of cold and hot nibbles, because it would be nice to be able to actually talk to your guests as well as put your head in and out of the oven.

Remember, people often find a particular canapé they like, so there is no need to make lots of different kinds. Smoked-salmon-based ones are always popular, as are anything with prawns or little sausages. There should be some vegetarian numbers available, too, but I have never found they go down a storm with a whole party. Do yourself a favour, though, and don't be too ambitious: whilst dinky miniature Yorkshire puddings with rare beef and horseradish are just to die for, you do have at least 200 canapés or so to get sorted *and* then at least try to look serene and vaguely welcoming to your dear guests as they arrive.

Possible options:

CREAMY AND CHEESY OR FRAGRANT THAI CRAB CANAPÉS

GOOEY MUSHROOM MOUTHFULS

VIETNAMESE DUCK WRAPS

CROSTINI WITH PRAWNS AND SWEET CHILLI SAUCE

SMOKED SALMON BLINIS WITH SOURED CREAM AND CHIVES

HONEYED SAUSAGES WITH MUSTARD MAYONNAISE

ASPARAGUS SPEARS WRAPPED IN PARMA HAM AND SERVED WITH A CHEESE FONDUE DIP

Creamy and Cheesy Crab Canapés

You could make two sorts of these: one creamy and cheesy with a cayenne bite; the other, rather more fragrant. You will need some of those Rahms mini croustades, which are sweet, ready-made, baby pastry cases. Oh, and tinned crabmeat is fine here.

Whichever canapé you make, force yourself to cool these delectable little bites just slightly before consuming with appropriate avarice.

2 x 170g tins white crabmeat
6 tablespoons double cream
4 tablespoons Parmesan cheese,
    finely grated

juice of 2 lemons
salt and pepper
24–32 Rahms mini croustades
cayenne pepper

Preheat the oven to 190°C/Gas Mark 5. Empty the tins of crabmeat into a sieve to drain them of their water. In a small bowl, combine the crabmeat with all the other ingredients except the cayenne pepper (and the mini croustades!) to form a gloopy mess. Using a teaspoon, fill the mini croustades with the mixture. Sprinkle a smidgen of cayenne pepper on top, then place them on a baking tray and cook for 8 minutes or until the pastry is crisp and its contents are bubbling.

makes about 24

Fragrant Thai Crab Canapés

2 x 170g tins white crabmeat
2 red onions, peeled and finely
   chopped
juice of 2 limes
2 tablespoons coriander, chopped

6 tablespoons good-quality
   mayonnaise
about 6 drops Tabasco sauce
2 teaspoons Thai fish sauce
24–32 Rahms mini croustades

Preheat the oven to 190°C/Gas Mark 5. Empty the tins of crabmeat into a sieve to drain them of their water, and combine the meat well with the other ingredients (again, except the mini croustades). Using a teaspoon, carefully stuff the cases, then place them on a baking tray and cook to perfection for 8 minutes.

makes about 24

Gooey Mushroom Mouthfuls

These are very easy to make and, if you are as greedy as me, you will find them exceptionally easy to eat, too.

40 chestnut mushrooms   **40 sprigs of thyme**
13 baby plum tomatoes   **black pepper**
1 Chaource cheese, or similar

I currently adore Chaource cheese, with its beautiful milky whiteness and earthy, almost mushroomy undertones. If you can't find this (but I exhort you to try, and I know Waitrose sells it), then use some white goat's cheese or Camembert instead. Take out the mushroom stalks and chop them finely. Then slice the baby plum tomatoes into 3 and pop one of the thirds into the base of each mushroom.

Top with a slice of the delicious cheese – not too much as you want it to fit inside the mushroom. Cover this with a sprinkling of mushroom stalks, a little sprig of thyme and some freshly ground black pepper. Slide them onto a baking tray and put them in the oven at 200°C/Gas Mark 6 for 10 minutes. Then stuff that gooey, molten mushroom in your mouth.

makes 20

Vietnamese Duck Wraps

When I made these they went down an absolute storm. It's hardly a recipe; it's merely a suggestion of how to imitate your local Vietnamese; cocktail-style. You could also make these as bigger, lunch-sized sandwiches. But, as far as I am concerned, diminutive and dinky has a particular appeal.

1 organic duck
7 packs soft tortilla wraps
2 x 150ml jars hoi sin sauce

8 spring onions, finely sliced into 3cm lengths
1 head of celery, thoroughly cleaned and finely sliced into 3cm lengths

A word of advice: if you are a make-up wearing sort of person, cook the duck before putting your slap on. A duck in the oven produces some smoke in the kitchen. Not good if you are wearing non-waterproof mascara. I'd still opt for cooking one over buying one ready-made. But if you fancy the easy option of buying in a duck all done and dusted, do feel free to do that. If you are cooking from scratch, place ducky on a rack over a roasting tin. You may want to pop some potatoes in the tin to gobble as a sneaky treat. But you will still need to drain off some fat, which will be wonderful for roasting future potatoes and parsnips for all your vegetarian friends. (Sorry, that just slipped out and I heartily take it back. Bad Elisa, bad Elisa …) A duck of around 2.5kg should take about 1½ hours at 200°C/Gas Mark 6.

Anyway, once the duck is cool, shred it and put the meat in a bowl. You won't need the skin, but if any of it is nicely crispy I won't look if you have a little nibble. Warm the tortillas as per the instructions on the packet, and now it's simply an assembly job. Smear the wrap quite thinly with some of the sauce (you don't want it oozing out and you probably won't use all of it). Now sprinkle about a tablespoon of duck meat in a horizontal line in the middle of the tortilla. Scatter with some of the spring onion and celery, remembering you have 7 tortillas to fill. Now roll up the tortilla from the bottom and wrap the top over to get a tight, long roll. Cut the tortilla into about 7 bite-sized pieces, discarding the ends if they have missed out on filling. Arrange the wraps standing upright, so their contents are enticingly on display.

makes about 50 bites

Crostini with Prawns and Sweet Chilli Sauce

Ideally, you want to use a baguette called a *ficelle* here, which is very skinny and makes far daintier croûtes than the normal-sized versions. If you can't find any, just get hold of the skinniest baguette you can find. A *ficelle* will make around 30 crostini, depending on the length of the loaf.

1 *ficelle* or similar thin baguette
olive oil, for brushing (optional)
1 x 200ml pot crème fraîche

60 large freshwater prawns, cooked
1 x 150ml jar sweet chilli sauce

Preheat the oven to 200°C/Gas Mark 6. Cut the bread into slices around ³/₄cm thick until you get 30 pieces. In fact, do prepare them the day before the party, or even before that, to save yourself a bit of time. Brush the bread with a little olive oil, if you wish (I didn't bother), place them on a baking sheet and pop them in the oven. Check them after 5 minutes, and don't leave the kitchen. You want them crisp and golden and not at all singed. Feel free to use the whole loaf, as the crostini can be stored in an airtight box. Leave them to cool and, shortly before the party kicks off, pile each crostini with a ½ teaspoon crème fraîche (or maybe more, depending on the size of the bread), a couple of prawns and a dab of the chilli sauce. Engagingly simple, they look a real treat.

other ideas for crostini
Houmous topped with a slice of black olive (see the recipe for houmous on page 213).

Guacamole topped with lightly cooked tuna steak (see the recipe for both on page 83).

makes about 30

Smoked Salmon Blinis with Soured Cream and Chives

You could make your own blinis, but, frankly, I wouldn't.

200g smoked salmon
40 ready-made cocktail-sized blinis
1 x 200ml pot soured cream or
    crème fraîche

black pepper
small bunch of chives (about 3–4
    tablespoons), finely chopped

Cut the salmon into squares just slightly bigger than the blinis. Heat the blinis through, according to the instructions on the packet, then fold a salmon square on top of each one when warm. Top with a little dollop of the soured cream or crème fraîche, a grinding of black pepper and a little sprinkle of chives.

other ideas for blinis
Soured cream with salmon keta or caviar (real or otherwise).

Flaked hot-smoked trout mixed with horseradish cream (see page 90 – just serve the trout cold and top with finely chopped chives).

Chopped herring with mayonnaise mixed with chopped dill.

Honeyed Sausages with Mustard Mayonnaise

Here's an easy way of providing hot and tasty fare with little trouble. These sausages are also somehow more filling than some of the other offerings. The Vicar always has an inbred need for hot food on any occasion, and if he were at your lovely do, he'd certainly be grateful for some of these.

60 good-quality cocktail sausages
enough runny honey to coat
4 garlic cloves, peeled and crushed

1 x 180g jar good-quality
**   mayonnaise**
¹/₂ x 180g jar wholegrain mustard

Preheat the oven to 160°C/Gas Mark 3. Put the sausages in a large roasting tin and drizzle over the honey. Mix in the crushed garlic and put the tray into the oven for about 30 minutes – but do check them as it's hard to be precise as to how long they will take, there being so many of them. Meanwhile, in a small serving bowl, mix the mayonnaise with the mustard and put it in the middle of a big round platter. Surround with the sausages, speared with cocktail sticks.

Asparagus Spears Wrapped in Parma Ham with a Cheese Fondue Dip

Do serve some breadsticks with this, too, to dip in the cheese fondue. (The recipe for the cheese fondue dip is on page 138.) Wheel this one out at the start of the evening, as the fondue needs stirring until it is ready and then needs to be eaten – fast.

40 baby asparagus, or thin asparagus spears, trimmed
40 slices of good Parma ham

salt and pepper
1 packet breadsticks

Steam or boil the asparagus spears for 3–5 minutes, depending on the thickness of the spears. You don't want them to be crunchy crisp, nor soggy, but just to have a little 'bite' to them. Drain and leave until cool enough to handle, then wrap each spear in a slice of Parma ham (just use half a slice if it looks too thick) and season well. Serve the fondue in a warmed bowl set on a platter with the asparagus and the breadsticks surrounding it.

And now, pop the Champagne: the party can begin …

makes 40

Index